SOCIAL ISSUES
FIRSTHAND

Eating Disorders

Other Books in the Social Issues Firsthand Series:

SOCIAL ISSUES
FIRSTHAND

Eating Disorders

Norah Piehl, Book Editor

GREENHAVEN PRESS
A part of Gale, Cengage Learning

GALE
CENGAGE Learning™

Detroit • New York • San Francisco • New Haven, Conn • Waterville, Maine • London

GALE
CENGAGE Learning

Christine Nasso, *Publisher*
Elizabeth Des Chenes, *Managing Editor*

© 2009 Greenhaven Press, a part of Gale, Cengage Learning.

Gale and Greenhaven Press are registered trademarks used herein under license.

For more information, contact:
Greenhaven Press
27500 Drake Rd.
Farmington Hills, MI 48331-3535
Or you can visit our Internet site at gale.cengage.com

For product information and technology assistance, contact us at

Gale Customer Support, 1-800-877-4253
For permission to use material from this text or product, submit all requests online at
www.cengage.com/permissions

Further permissions questions can be emailed to permissionrequest@cengage.com

Articles in Greenhaven Press anthologies are often edited for length to meet page requirements. In addition, original titles of these works are changed to clearly present the main thesis and to explicitly indicate the author's opinion. Every effort is made to ensure that Greenhaven Press accurately reflects the original intent of the authors. Every effort has been made to trace the owners of copyrighted material.

Cover image copyright Amy Walters, 2008. Used under license from Shutterstock.com.

LIBRARY OF CONGRESS CATALOGING-IN-PUBLICATION DATA

Eating disorders / Norah Piehl, book editor.
    p. cm. -- (Social issues firsthand)
    Includes bibliographical references and index.
    ISBN 978-0-7377-4252-7 (hardcover)
    1. Eating disorders--Popular works. I. Piehl, Norah.
    RC552.E18E2821135 2008
    616.85'26--dc22

                                                            2008028511

Printed in the United States of America
1 2 3 4 5 6 7 12 11 10 09 08

Contents

Chapter 1: A Broad Spectrum of Illness

Chapter 2: Family Connections

Foreword

Social issues are often viewed in abstract terms. Pressing challenges such as poverty, homelessness, and addiction are viewed as problems to be defined and solved. Politicians, social scientists, and other experts engage in debates about the extent of the problems, their causes, and how best to remedy them. Often overlooked in these discussions is the human dimension of the issue. Behind every policy debate over poverty, homelessness, and substance abuse, for example, are real people struggling to make ends meet, to survive life on the streets, and to overcome addiction to drugs and alcohol. Their stories are ubiquitous and compelling. They are the stories of everyday people—perhaps your own family members or friends—and yet they rarely influence the debates taking place in state capitols, the national Congress, or the courts.

The disparity between the public debate and private experience of social issues is well illustrated by looking at the topic of poverty. Each year the U.S. Census Bureau establishes a poverty threshold. A household with an income below the threshold is defined as poor, while a household with an income above the threshold is considered able to live on a basic subsistence level. For example, in 2003 a family of two was considered poor if its income was less than $12,015; a family of four was defined as poor if its income was less than $18,810. Based on this system, the bureau estimates that 35.9 million Americans (12.5 percent of the population) lived below the poverty line in 2003, including 12.9 million children below the age of eighteen.

Commentators disagree about what these statistics mean. Social activists insist that the huge number of officially poor Americans translates into human suffering. Even many families that have incomes above the threshold, they maintain, are likely to be struggling to get by. Other commentators insist that the statistics exaggerate the problem of poverty in the United States. Compared to people in developing countries, they point out, most so-called poor families have a high quality of life. As stated by journalist Fidelis Iyebote, "Cars are owned by 70 percent of 'poor' households. . . . Color televisions belong to 97 percent of the 'poor' [and] videocassette recorders belong to nearly 75 percent. . . . Sixty-four percent have microwave ovens, half own a stereo system, and over a quarter possess an automatic dishwasher."

However, this debate over the poverty threshold and what it means is likely irrelevant to a person living in poverty. Simply put, poor people do not need the government to tell them whether they are poor. They can see it in the stack of bills they cannot pay. They are aware of it when they are forced to choose between paying rent or buying food for their children. They become painfully conscious of it when they lose their homes and are forced to live in their cars or on the streets. Indeed, the written stories of poor people define the meaning of poverty more vividly than a government bureaucracy could ever hope to. Narratives composed by the poor describe losing jobs due to injury or mental illness, depict horrific tales of childhood abuse and spousal violence, recount the loss of friends and family members. They evoke the slipping away of social supports and government assistance, the descent into substance abuse and addiction, the harsh realities of life on the streets. These are the perspectives on poverty that are too often omitted from discussions over the extent of the problem and how to solve it.

Greenhaven Press's *Social Issues Firsthand* series provides a forum for the often-overlooked human perspectives on society's most divisive topics of debate. Each volume focuses on one social issue and presents a collection of ten to sixteen narratives by those who have had personal involvement with the topic. Extra care has been taken to include a diverse range of perspectives. For example, in the volume on adoption, readers will find the stories of birth parents who have made an adoption plan, adoptive parents, and adoptees themselves. After exposure to these varied points of view, the reader will have a clearer understanding that adoption is an intense, emotional experience full of joyous highs and painful lows for all concerned.

The debate surrounding embryonic stem cell research illustrates the moral and ethical pressure that the public brings to bear on the scientific community. However, while nonexperts often criticize scientists for not considering the potential negative impact of their work, ironically the public's reaction against such discoveries can produce harmful results as well. For example, although the outcry against embryonic stem cell research in the United States has resulted in fewer embryos being destroyed, those with Parkinson's, such as actor Michael J. Fox, have argued that prohibiting the development of new stem cell lines ultimately will prevent a timely cure for the disease that is killing Fox and thousands of others.

Each book in the series contains several features that enhance its usefulness, including an in-depth introduction, an annotated table of contents, bibliographies for further research, a list of organizations to contact, and a thorough index. These elements—combined with the poignant voices of people touched by tragedy and triumph—make the *Social Issues Firsthand* series a valuable resource for research on today's topics of political discussion.

Introduction

Male Athletes, Body Image, and Disordered Eating

Public service announcements, articles indicting the fashion industry for perpetuating an unrealistic body image, and memoirs written by celebrities and others have all contributed to raising public awareness about eating disorders. These media messages, however, have also perpetuated the widely held belief that disordered eating is overwhelmingly a "women's disease." Although it is true that females represent the vast majority of cases in eating disorder treatment clinics, many men and adolescent boys are at risk of developing distorted eating and exercise patterns, even if their symptoms never become severe enough, or if sociological pressures never become strong enough, for them to seek treatment.

Although the eating habits and body weight of too-thin actresses and models have long been scrutinized, in recent years, numerous articles have discussed the dangerous prevalence of eating disorders among women athletes, including cheerleaders, dancers, gymnasts, and figure skaters. Noted Olympic female athletes, including gymnasts Nadia Comaneci and Cathy Rigby and diver Kimiko Harai Soldati, have made their struggles with anorexia and bulimia public in an effort to raise awareness. Although several recent studies have indicated that all athletes—regardless of gender—might be at higher risk for eating disorders than the general population, the existence of disordered eating among male athletes has received almost no publicity. Male athletes' eating disorders are in many ways similar to females', but significant differences in the ways men and boys view their bodies and approach sports present challenges to acknowledging, diagnosing, and treating their disordered eating.

Male Athletes and Body Image: The Adonis Complex

For girls and women, one of the largest components affecting their eating and exercise patterns—and leading, in some cases, to eating disorders—is the overwhelming desire for thinness. Although most prevalent in appearance-conscious sports such as figure-skating, cheerleading, and gymnastics, the drive for thinness appears to be a near-universal motivating factor among women athletes, even those (like basketball and tennis players) for whom thinness is not a prerequisite for athletic success. In fact, most female athletes surveyed in a landmark 1999 study of NCAA Division I athletes responded that they would aspire to a very thin body type with less than 13 percent body fat, despite the fact that this shape would result in the absence of menstruation and possibly in the early onset of osteoporosis.

Men and boys, however, aspire to a very different ideal body type, characterized by a well-developed upper body and narrow waist and hips, as well as a high percentage of lean muscle mass and low body fat—the kind of body sported by models that grace the cover of increasingly popular magazines such as *Men's Health* and *Men's Fitness*. This "supermale" standard, with its well-defined abdominal and pectoral muscles, is the subject of what Harrison G. Pope and others have dubbed the "Adonis Complex" or "muscular dysphoria," a drive for a body shape just as unrealistic for most men as the ultra-thin body type is for most women.

As a result of this pressure to achieve an impractical body shape, disordered eating in male athletes often takes the form not of self-starvation (anorexia) or bingeing and purging (bulimia), but rather of binge eating, excessive exercise, erratic eating, overuse of nutritional supplements, or even abuse of steroids and other muscle-enhancing drugs. Many of these symptoms, even in combination, fail to meet established psychiatric standards for eating disorders, and consequently go unrecognized and underreported.

Which Male Athletes Are at Risk?

Like female athletes, men involved in appearance-conscious sports (such as gymnastics and figure skating), sports in which a very lean body is considered athletically advantageous (such as cycling, distance running, and swimming), and sports with weight classes (such as horse racing, wrestling, and crew) are considered particularly high-risk for developing eating disorders. In male athletes, body dissatisfaction (and the resultant risk for eating disorders) is particularly high when an athletic body type that might excel in a given sport still fails to measure up to the Adonis ideal. In one study in the journal *Adolescence*, high school male cross-country runners, who tend to be lean and light, expressed much higher body dissatisfaction—and higher rates of disordered eating—than football players, whose body shapes as a whole matched up better to the ideal. Societal and peer pressure to achieve not only excellence in a given sport but also a sometimes-contradictory ideal shape seems to set up certain male athletes even more for risky eating and exercise patterns.

Looking the Other Way

As noted above, men, even those who are surveyed about eating disorders as part of standard admissions practices in college sports programs, are often overlooked because their patterns of disordered eating and exercise are not picked up in standard screenings for anorexia and bulimia. In addition, the symptoms of men with disordered eating—which often include long hours at the gym and in the weight room, far above and beyond ordinary training regimens—can be viewed by many of their peers and coaches as admirable, even exemplary. Male athletes' eating disorders also tend to be cyclical, as men (often as part of a team bonding activity) diet excessively or binge and purge prior to the start of a competitive season, only to return to more normal eating patterns in the off-season. All these elements combine to make men's disordered eating less easily identifiable and treatable.

Finally, given the public perception of eating disorders as women's concerns, men may be reluctant to acknowledge a problem publicly, even if they suspect one exists. Suffering from what's perceived as a feminine disease is particularly threatening to men who may, after all, have developed their disorder in the pursuit of an ultramasculine ideal.

New Approaches

Of course, one of the best ways to counter this perception would be to publicize men's eating disorders. A handful of men, including athletes, have stepped forward to acknowledge the problem publicly, and new publications and organizations should continue to help bring public awareness to these little-understood, but very real, disorders.

Many studies advocate incorporating eating disorders prevention into training plans for college and elite athletes, male and female alike. Involving a health administrator (to monitor diet and exercise) or a psychiatrist onto the training team, along with coaches, personal trainers, and nutritionists, could help bring conversations about disordered eating and exercise out of the closet and prevent problems before they start. Coaches and athletic trainers also need better education to help them recognize at-risk athletes, even those whose symptoms might not fall under strict clinical definitions for eating disorders.

Ultimately, though, little about this problem will change until the public becomes more aware of the differences between normal and disordered eating, particularly among male athletes. As more and more amateur athletes train for endurance sports such as long-distance cycling and marathon running, for example, it seems likely that nonelite athletes who don't have the benefit of a professional training team will continue to suffer from disordered eating and exercise patterns in secret. Publicizing the existence of the problem, celebrating athletes of all shapes and sizes, and listening to the stories of men who have overcome disordered eating will all go a long way toward combating what has become a near-silent syndrome.

SOCIAL ISSUES
FIRSTHAND

CHAPTER 1

A Broad Spectrum of Illness

Ballet Dancing Led Me
to Anorexia

Lana D'Amico

As a teenager, Lana D'Amico was a serious ballet student. She studied under one of the top teachers in the business and devoted virtually all of her free time to dance. For a while, D'Amico was able to achieve a balance between dance excellence and a healthy body. But during an intensive summer dance program when she was seventeen, D'Amico drastically cut her food intake, and developed an eating disorder that she reluctantly labels as anorexia.

In her article, D'Amico discusses the circumstances that led to her eating disorder and describes her long recovery process, one that she argues actually made her a stronger and better dancer. D'Amico reminds readers that despite many misconceptions, an emaciated body type is not normal or essential for female ballet dancers, and that excessive thinness actually impairs athletic and artistic performance.

Following her time as a serious dance student, Lana D'Amico has pursued a career in writing and publishing. She was an intern for Dance Magazine *and has since written articles for various women's magazines.*

I'm not sure when it started. What I *do* know is that it *wasn't* about being thin enough for a guy, or about not being happy in my life, and it certainly wasn't because I thought I was fat. For "real" life, I knew that I was fine. But for ballet, I wasn't quite thin enough, or so I believed.

I'd wanted to be a ballerina for as long as I could remember. While most teens were at the mall, dating, or getting that perfect prom dress. I was at ballet. Ballet class wasn't just something I went to for fun; it was my whole life. When I wasn't at dance, I was watching videos of my favorites, listening to classical music and envisioning choreography, or daydreaming about being onstage.

Defining Myself

To this day, I have a hard time saying that I was anorexic. I certainly wasn't bulimic. But while I may not have starved myself completely or binged and purged, I definitely had some serious issues about food. I suppose that anorexia is the closest description to what I put myself through.

I hear stories about girls whose teachers demand that they get thin, but my ballet teacher, Frank Ohman—a wonderfully talented man who had been a soloist in the New York City Ballet—did *not* encourage me to lose weight. He actually called my mother once, to ask if I was unwell. "She looked fine before," he told her. "Lana's getting too thin now—and it's happened really fast. I'm concerned." I can't ever recall Mr. Ohman putting anyone down because of their weight. Like a true professional, he was more concerned with ability, potential, and one's level of desire to be there.

Even though my mom got annoyed at me and may have been a little embarrassed about the call, I didn't think too much about it.

A Sudden Change

Then, when I was about 17, and deeply focused on a professional career, my once-curvy figure became a thing of the past. My legs were like those of most dancers: a mass of muscles. But the rest of me was skin and bones. My ribcage was completely visible from front to back. My arms looked as though they'd snap, and my face looked way too large for the rest of me.

In 1995, I got accepted to the Richmond Ballet's summer dance program. Faced with competing against talented dancers from all across the country, I was mentally and physically pushed to the limit. I worked hard in Virginia, and cut my intake of food down to one meal a day. I would dance from ten in the morning until six at night; eating only once—sounds insane, right?

That summer, I stopped getting my period. Instead of becoming alarmed, though, I knew it meant I was losing weight. I'd arrived in Virginia at 5'4" and 110 pounds. By the time I left, I weighed a mere 98 pounds.

"Something Was Wrong"

Although I'd learned a lot in my time away, I was eager to come home, see my friends and family, and rest. I can still recall what went through my mind as I took my bow in our final workshop performance—*I don't want to dance; I'm tired.*

I thought my dancing was stronger, but overall, I was exhausted. When my parents came to get me, they were worried. Through happy tears at seeing me for the first time in a few months, my mom said, "You look terrible."

At this point, I knew something was wrong. For the first time, I looked in the mirror and saw what I *really* looked like. Back at home, my friends said, "What happened to you? Did you not eat a bite the whole summer?"

Not exactly flattering. I wanted to shout, "But you should see how much better I've gotten!"

Slow Improvement

I knew I had to eat normally and snap out of it. I was tired of hurting my parents and myself. My mother talked of taking me to see a therapist if I didn't get back to a normal eating pattern. I panicked—I didn't want that! So, very slowly, I began to eat a little more, to respond better to my hunger rather than suppressing it. Because I always ate dinner with my parents, they didn't know how little I was eating at other times. I'd be voracious at dinner with them, therefore presenting a seemingly healthy appetite.

Once I started eating properly again—wouldn't you know it? My dancing got better! With more energy, I was better able to attack steps and not be completely beat after classes and rehearsals. When I began to menstruate again, I knew that I was finally back on track. Three months without a menstrual period can be hazardous to one's health, especially for a growing girl.

Trying to Measure Up

When I think back, I realize what the problem stemmed from. There's a lot of pressure on young girls. We feel that we need to look a certain way to fit a particular mold. For me, that mold was what I perceived as "the ballerina look." For others, it's something else. Let me say that many ballerinas do *not* look anorexic. Sure, there are some—but it's nearly impossible to maintain such a low body weight and still have the stamina that ballet demands.

Instead of shedding a pound or two, I lost control and lost sight of what I really looked like. I was obsessed with being reed-thin, and didn't realize that I'd be too tired to achieve my original goal. It doesn't matter how skinny you look in your costume if you're too tired to dance with the necessary bravura. I consider myself lucky, though. I was able to gain control of my eating before it became even more of a problem for me.

What I Learned

Sometimes I remind myself of what happened. With the pressures of a professional ballet career behind me now, I have to say I feel better in my skin. Oh, I still daydream about what could have been, and I wouldn't take back one minute of practice for anything in the world. I've continued dancing for the pure love of it, and I still adore going to the ballet.

The regimen of dance taught me about concentration, passion, goals, dedication, and plain old hard work. My ballet mentor and I are still good friends, and when I pop into his class he's happy to see that I look healthy. And when my parents get on my case about something, I listen.

My Struggle with Bulimia

Kathryn, as told to Sandy Fertman Ryan

Kathryn, who was seventeen when she told her story to author Sandy Fertman Ryan, grew up in a high-achieving family. Kathryn always had set lofty goals for herself too, including achieving academic success and popularity. But as Kathryn entered her teenage years, she turned her perfectionism to a new target: her body.

As a boarding school student, Kathryn admired the personal control of an anorexic friend; when she began to struggle with her own weight gain, she turned to purging to control her weight. Kathryn's ongoing struggle with bulimia went on for months, resulting in two suicide attempts. Only when Kathryn, with the help of experts at an eating disorders clinic, began to deal with the psychological roots of her bulimia, was she able to develop a healthier attitude toward eating, fitness, and body image, and to create a more balanced portrait of her own self-worth.

Sandy Fertman Ryan writes for the magazine Girls' Life.

Although I grew up in an extremely nice home in Berkeley, California, with my parents and two little brothers, I wouldn't say I had a normal childhood. My parents are pretty high-powered—my dad is a successful international lawyer, and my mom is a systems analyst. They are the ultimate perfectionists, so they raised me to be an overachiever in everything I did. This is how bad it was: When I was 5, my aunt offered to take me to see *Beauty and the Beast*. I told her I couldn't go because "my schedule was too tight."

My whole life, I've tried to be No. 1 at everything. I was one of the best players on my soccer team, I always got the highest grades in school, and I was extremely popular. But even with all that, I never felt I was good enough.

Need for Control

I grew up believing that, to be beautiful, you have to be thin. No surprise, my mom was super-skinny. In seventh grade, I became overweight and just hated my body. Soon, I made it my goal to get thin.

By the end of seventh grade, I was dying to get away from Berkeley and from my parents because they were so overly critical of my body and everything else I did. So they agreed to let me attend boarding school in England. At first, it was really exciting—the school was so interesting, and I met some amazing people. But after a short while, the academic challenge was gone, and I was totally bored and unhappy.

One of my friends at the school was anorexic. Although I hated to watch what she was doing to herself, at the same time, I was secretly impressed with how she was mastering her body. It wasn't long before another girl at school told me how she purged so she wouldn't have to diet. I honestly thought to myself, "That is so cool!"

That November, I visited my parents, who were living in Paris temporarily. They decided that, since I was so unhappy in England, I should attend an international school in Paris. I was only 14 but, after being academically tested, I was advanced to the 11th grade. That was so difficult, because everyone in my class was between 17 and 19 years old! I became totally overwhelmed by the pressure, and I quickly gained another 10 pounds. That's when I decided to try purging as a way of getting a handle on my weight. I remember having such a sense of power the first time I put my fingers down my throat. Finally, I had control over my body.

"I Can't Stop"

My parents found out about my vomiting two weeks later, when they noticed some remnants in the toilet. They said,

"Kathryn, we're so disappointed. You have to snap out of it!" That only made me feel more alienated. I knew my problem went much deeper—and I knew I couldn't stop myself. I was just totally stressed out trying to be older than I was and, at the same time, still shooting for perfection. I purged to feel like I had control over something in my life, since everything else seemed to be totally out of control.

Soon, I was purging about five times a day—at home, school, clubs, parties, wherever. I'd just turn on the water in the bathroom to mask the sound of my vomiting, and then I'd wash my face and chew gum to refresh my breath. But I was miserable. Binging and purging actually had control over me rather than the other way around. My teeth became discolored because of the acid from my vomit, and I developed a scar around the knuckle of my index finger from constantly sticking my finger down my throat.

My parents sent me to a psychiatrist, who prescribed antidepressants. That turned out to be horrible for me. I had a reverse reaction to the drugs and ended up getting more anxious than before. Little did anyone know I was entering the scariest phase of my illness—I was having frequent thoughts of killing myself. That's how desperate I felt.

Falling Apart

In March, my mom moved with me back to England. She felt I should go back to the boarding school. One afternoon, I got a knife from the kitchen to slit my wrists when, luckily, my mom came home. I was crying uncontrollably and I told her I couldn't deal with my life anymore. I'd completely fallen apart. I told her I felt like a failure and that I was willing to do anything to get better.

My parents immediately sent me back to California for a weeklong eating disorders program at Stanford University. I was 15 by that time. Basically, the doctors' tactic was to scare me into quitting my purging by explaining what it was doing to my body. They told my parents I was on the verge of heart failure due to all the damage I'd caused my body. To top it off, my hair was thinning and my throat was bleeding. The treatment helped, and I stopped purging altogether.

I repeated my junior year in Berkeley, while continuing to see a therapist. Although I was really popular and kept up a straight-A average, my intense self-pressure kicked in once again and, after two months, I was vomiting again. Every time I purged, I hated myself, feeling so ashamed and alone.

One day, after a horrible binge, I was in my room crying and depressed and thought, "I can't deal with this anymore!" I was so distraught and felt like no one noticed how miserable I was. So I went into my mom's bathroom and took a bottle of pills in an attempt to kill myself. But then I freaked, thinking, "I don't want to die!" My mom was downstairs, so I screamed for her. She gave me some medicine that caused me to throw up the pills, then took me to the hospital.

The "Perfect" Ending

Shortly after my attempted suicide, my parents sent me to The Center, an eating disorders clinic in Washington. By then, I had turned 16. The therapists made me feel really good about myself, because I could talk out my problems. Finally, it hit home that losing weight wasn't ever going to give me what I really needed—self-worth.

Gradually, I stopped purging. I learned to eat better, take vitamins and work out. Now, I'm much stronger, physically and mentally. Sure, there are still days I get really sad and am hard on myself, but not at all like before. I haven't purged for months now. I think what really healed me was recognizing that I can't possibly achieve everything I want to achieve if I continue to be sick with bulimia. In fact, I probably wouldn't have even survived if I had kept it up.

Over time, I figured out that my problem wasn't about being thin—it was that I wanted to be accepted and loved unconditionally. I know my parents love me, but they've always been way too critical of me. I really think that's why I was trying to control my weight—I wanted to be perfect so that maybe, just maybe, I'd be lovable to them. Now, I finally believe that I am lovable just by being me and that it never mattered how perfect—or imperfect—I was.

Overcoming Compulsive Eating

Frances Kuffel

Most experts classify compulsive eating as a type of eating disorder. Frances Kuffel would certainly agree with them. In this article, she describes how first her compulsive eating, and then her highly publicized extreme weight loss, resulted in a sense of self that was totally centered on her body. Kuffel reflects that after her dramatic weight loss, she viewed herself solely as a number—her dress size. When she gained even a little weight, stress, unrealistic expectations, and low self-esteem quickly escalated, leading her down the path of her old self-destructive compulsive eating habits.

Kuffel's essay speaks to a holistic, realistic approach to healing eating disorders, one which treats the whole person and doesn't view each slipup as a complete failure. She anchors her compulsive eating behavior in larger personal issues and discovers that she needs to address those concerns along with maintaining a healthy attitude toward food and her body.

Frances Kuffel's dramatic weight loss story was publicized in the pages of O: The Oprah Magazine, *among other media outlets. Her book documenting her weight loss is* Passing for Thin: Losing Half My Weight and Finding Myself. *She is currently at work on a project titled* Angry Fat Girls.

I had been summoned to The Show, the Holy Grail for authors and the fulfillment of all my mother's dreams. In a harried day of phone calls from Chicago, at the tail end of a snowstorm, the producers of *Oprah* decided, with 90 minutes to catch the last shuttle out of LaGuardia, that they might want me.

You'd think, on the eve of what could catapult my book to national attention, that I would be too nervous to eat.

I am never too nervous to eat.

As I grazed the basket of goodies in my expensed suite, I had two questions. First: Would Harpo Productions' bean counters go over my hotel tab and ask, "Isn't that the woman who lost all that weight? What are these charges for chocolate-covered almonds and honey peanuts doing here?"

Second: Why am I eating all this stuff? I might be on TV tomorrow!

What with *Oprah* replaying 24/7, everyone in America could count the bread crumbs on my velvet dress.

Ready for the Big Time?

So much for the can-do kid who, after 42 years of obesity and missed opportunities, had lost 188 pounds and written a book about it. *Passing for Thin: Losing Half My Weight and Finding My Self* is an account of how I used my radical change in weight to turn a small, private world of eating and surviving into one as big as my former size 32 dresses. I climbed mountains! I swaddled myself in cashmere and had lovers; I went to Italy. I floated out of the gym after lifting weights, I sat in restaurant booths, wore bracelets, and crossed my legs and took the middle seat in airplanes. Then I used my weight loss to do the next impossible thing: I became an author. Being thin opened the doors to experience and intimacy.

National exposure, however, was an intrusion I hadn't considered. I am not a pundit or role model. You're going to be pilloried [publicly ridiculed], Frances, I thought with the vehemence of a Sicilian curse.

And yet, there I was gobbling Oprah's $12 cookies.

I put on my pajamas and pulled back the comforter on the king-size bed. It was littered with wrappers. My cheeks were burning with shame and calories. Tomorrow, I promised myself solemnly.

And when tomorrow came, I smiled and joked, and I was gracious when I wasn't, after all, needed for the show. I ached not from disappointment but with the hangover of sugar in my muscles, the sour gas in my gut and the heartbreak of being a liar.

A Relapse

After a failed romance and a change of jobs, I drifted into relapse in March 2003, a year before *Oprah*. I had time on my hands—and time, in my case, is the enemy. I filled it by studying where and how I went wrong, at the office, in the bedroom. Intellectually, I knew that the boyfriend was emotionally frozen and that my former employer was abusive and infantilizing, but I couldn't shake my ingrained conviction that I was responsible for everything that went wrong.

I stopped going to the gym; I started eating peanuts or rice cakes between meals. A little of this, a little of that, and one morning I announced to a friend that I saw no reason why I couldn't eat blackberry pie and ice cream, get the craving out of my system and return to my abstinence by noon.

I wasn't talking about a slice of pie à la mode. I was talking about a whole pie and a pint of ice cream.

A whole pie?

That summer I was reminded at every turn that I needed to be thin to promote my book. "You don't want those cookies, honey," my mom said as I carried off a stack I'd grabbed from the cooling rack. "Remember: You're going to be in Oprah's magazine."

She was wrong. I did want the cookies, and I didn't need reminding about *Oprah*. I sighed and took two more.

Endless Hungers

When I asked myself what I needed, I was met with an unconsoling barrage of hungers. I needed to know I was not disposable. I needed a resting place. I needed to know I had enough stuff to carry off the rest of my life—enough talent, discipline and intelligence—and enough sufficiency to protect me from more heartbreak. I needed enough hope to find the friends and man I mourned the lack of.

From August 1999 to August 2003, I'd gambled that losing weight would get me closer to all that, and I was told what to eat in those years. Now, after three years of maintaining my weight loss, I need to be told what to feel when everyone but me has an opinion of who I am.

I knew I—not just my body but my very self—was in trouble when I brushed aside a fleeting thought about how fat I looked with the answer, "Never mind. You'll like yourself when you're thin."

Finding Confidence

How does one live with self-acceptance as a future and an always-conditional state of mind? More pragmatically, in lieu of my size 8 clothes, my career depended on self-assurance. When asked, I admitted that I'd gained weight, adding that I had never presented myself as the poster girl of thin. I said this with poise, which is not to be confused with confidence. Poise is teachable; confidence is one of the elements missing from the periodic table, three parts self-respect to two parts experience.

To get to confidence, I was going to have to listen to my self-accusations and sit with the rejections. Maybe shame had something to teach me. My next recovery period from food addiction would be based on therapy, heretofore more a matter of coaching than peeling back the layers of self. My psychiatrist's and therapist's offices became the places I could air my feelings about myself in the hopes I could change my self-perception. "There's no point in getting depressed just because I'm depressed," I told my psychiatrist, who increased my morning meds anyway.

Broadening Identity

That October, on a blue-and-gold afternoon, I had Indian food with Lanie, a friend visiting from my hometown, Missoula, Montana. I described how depressed I was by my weight gain until she preempted me. "You've been very fat, Frances, and you've been very thin. Welcome to where the rest of us live."

I twiddled my fork in my plate of *saag panir*. I think of Lanie as being very tall and very thin, but a few months earlier I'd helped her pick out a dress. Her dress size was similar to what I was wearing that day. The event we shopped for had been a gathering of Montana writers, many of them old friends, all middle-aged. One had a rounder face than I remembered; another wore layers of a truly terrible print in the style that catalogs and store clerks describe as "flattering." Someone else was still very thin but looked drawn and brittle as age caught up with her bone structure.

These were women I'd long envied for their pretty thinness, and yet I'd been less like them when I was a size 8 than I was now.

At size 8, I had to admit, I was so self-conscious (and secretly, overweeningly proud of it) that often that was all I was. I could have programmed my answering machine to announce, "Hi, you've reached a size 8. Please leave a message and either the size 8 or Frances will get back to you."

None of the women at that party, or Lanie savoring her lamb kurma across from me, claimed their identities from their weights that night. They wanted to gossip, compare stories of their kids and discuss what they were writing, tell old jokes more cleverly than they had at the last party, and sample the desserts weighing down the potluck buffet.

Redefining Myself

I was not unlike them. Smaller by a size than Lanie, larger by a size than Laura, a little fresher looking than Diane. Of the

Americans who lose weight, 95 percent gain it back within five years. I had gained a third of it back. Not all of it. To some extent, I had beaten the odds. I was stronger than the echoes of the boyfriend and boss allowed me to hear.

I was determined not to repeat the mistake of being, rather than having, a thin body. I'd lived through my size all of my life, so acutely aware and ashamed of my obesity that the likable things about me—my sense of humor, my intelligence, talent, friendliness, kindness—were as illusory to me as a magician's stacked card deck. As long as I defined myself by my body size, I would not experience those qualities for myself.

As fall turned to a snowy winter, I picked through the spiral of relationships that had unglued me the year before. I didn't blame the boyfriend or my boss for my relapse. I had been half of the problem; healthier self-esteem would not have collapsed under their judgments of me. In obesity, I had clamped my arms to my sides to keep them from swinging as I walked. I craned my body over armrests in theaters and airplanes, stood in the back of group photos to minimize the space I took up. I got thin and I continued to hide. Whatever reasons the boyfriend had come up with for not seeing me, I met with amicability and sympathy. Had I reacted honestly, even to myself, I might have ended the relationship. Instead, I'd gambled all my sweetness only to find out I was disposable. Likewise, I had not pressed my boss for an agenda of responsibilities from the start, nor had I clarified with her that her work and recreation styles frustrated and frightened me.

Finding My Footing

Slowly, I began to find toeholds in the avalanche of food and doubt. I worried about how fat I looked to potential readers and what I could possibly wear to flatter or disguise the 40 pounds I'd gained.

At the same time, however, I had become the canvas of makeup artists, stylists, photographers and publicists. They weren't looking at my stomach. "Give me a hundred-watt smile," commanded a photographer whose censure I thought I'd seen when I walked in. I licked my teeth and flashed a grin only somewhat longer than her camera flare.

"Wow." She straightened up at the tripod. "That really is a hundred watts. These are gonna be great."

When I saw myself in the magazine, my smile was, in fact, the focal point. When I began dating, at the age of 45, my smile was an attribute men commented on, but I hadn't really seen it until it was emblazoned on glossy paper. It was bigger, it seemed, than my face itself. I'd been a size 8 in my author photo, taken as my food plan was wobbling but not yet in smithereens, in June 2003. I was surprised to see I still looked like myself, apparently.

"Tired of the Games"

The power of my smile fueled me through more publicity, giving me a sense of authentic attractiveness that allowed me to enjoy the process. When I had a couple of days in Santa Monica between readings, I had a chance to assess and absorb at my own pace. Walking along the Palisades, I admired the sea-twisted pines and pearly mist funneling out of Malibu Canyon. I felt as lucky as I had once felt by being hired, by being loved, and I felt worthy of my luck because I appreciated the prettiness of the place, the serendipity that brought me there and my particular grateful awareness that knitted the moment together. I'd tried to rob myself of that by punishing myself for the boss and the boyfriend. You should not have treated me that way, I thought. The emphasis was on "me," and just then I knew who that was.

I looked around carefully. There was a family reunion going on, or so I assumed until I got closer and realized it was a cookout hosted for the park's lost and unfound citizens. I smiled to myself. How California. No gritty, iron-shuttered Salvation Army outposts here, no soup and Jell-O punishment for being a bum. No siree Bob. In California, the homeless are just one more variant on the Beach Boys.

I laughed out loud. I'm here, I gloated. I like my own company.

I was tired of the games—with food, with hiding what I looked like under big clothes and my big smile, with waiting until I was a size 8 again to like myself.

A Happy Medium

I recommitted to chipping at my food addiction, but I let go of some of the rigidity I'd had in the first years of losing and maintaining my weight loss. "I want to be praised when I do things right, and I want to be forgiven when I mess up," I told the people closest to me. "And I want milk in my coffee."

It was a small list, but significant because it allowed me to fumble as I gained my momentum of eating sanely. Esteem, kindness, patience, forgiveness: By cloaking myself in these qualities, I could build a self that was not afraid of authority figures and charming men who have one eye on the door.

Maybe these attributes will curb the millions of things that make me want to eat, starting with seeing my parents or returning to Montana. I turn into the kid whose mother had to make her school uniform, whose big tummy stretched the plaid into an Escher cartoon; I become the sad, joking fat college student who was reading *The Faerie Queene* while her girlfriends were soaking up the half-naked wonder of being 20 years old. I think of my parents' kitchens, and my mouth waters for gingerbread and well-buttered toast.

Learning to Listen to Myself

I regress when I let people like Lanie, whose struggle is different, comment or take charge of what I eat.

"That's two entrees, Frances," Lanie pointed out when I said I wanted goat cheese salad and roast chicken for our first lunch together in Paris.

"Oh. Well, then, I'll have the salad I guess," I settled, grumpily. That's the way I eat, that's how I lost 188 pounds: vegetables and protein. I was allowing her to limit me to a smidgen of cheese, or insufficient vegetables, and allowing her supervision is how I got so mad—that fatal elixir of anger and crazed desire—that I bought all the chocolate in Charles De Gaulle [Paris airport] for my untasting delectation.

I am the kid who, when told not to put beans up her nose, heads directly to the pantry.

"I have got to learn to tell people to stay out of my food," I reported to my therapist back in New York.

Healing at My Own Pace

Then again, perhaps this is an evolutionary process rather than a one-time miracle cure. In 2003, I denned up for two months in Montana and ate. In 2004, I struggled again in Montana but I also did a lot of hiking, alone with my dog and with my niece. My slow pace didn't frustrate either of them. I went horseback riding and got a terrific tan while swimming every afternoon. My thighs did not chafe in the August heat along the Seine, and I was thrilled to cross the Appalachian Trail later that autumn. I had spells of disappointment and fear from the way I ate, but I was living in my body, on my body's terms.

It's a small world I've pulled from the wrappers, boxes and crumbs in the past two years, but a very human one. I've seen my family, close friends and therapists hold on to a stubborn belief that I would come through this. They loved me enough to countenance my mistakes and let me start over. Each day, I venture a little farther from the safety of food, and my courage comes from understanding that I am a lot like a lot of people—a family member, a friend, a dog owner, a recidivist, a middle-aged woman, a writer who got a good rhythm going and forgot to brush her hair. There is safety in numbers.

Depression and relapse would have to wait for a different excuse than my size.

I am ready to hope again.

My Battle with Anorexia and Schizophrenia

Candy Newman

Eating disorders are mental illnesses, and as such, they often exist hand in hand with other mental illnesses, such as depression. In the case of Candy Newman, her anorexia triggered the development of schizophrenia, a mental illness characterized by fractured thought processes and a distortion of reality. The author, for example, became convinced that one of her college professors had infected her with HIV, resulting in her extreme weight loss. In reality, Newman's extreme thinness was caused by an eating disorder, which in turn controlled her body and mind.

In this essay, which traces her long road to recovery, Newman argues that mental health professionals need to be better educated about the potential links between eating disorders and schizophrenia, particularly in women. Schizophrenia is relatively rare in women, leading several of the author's doctors to make incorrect or confused diagnoses. The author also discusses her eventual management of her mental health with prescription medications and admits that without drugs, she would probably have a relapse.

A graduate of York University in Canada, Candy Newman is now a writer and poet who lives with her husband in Toronto.

The thought that my teacher was not really talking about her plans to inject me with HIV did not seen implausible to me. So, what was wrong?

I eventually discovered it was schizophrenia. Schizophrenia is defined as a break from reality. It involves a disruption in thinking patterns, such as with concentration, memory, disor-

Candy Newman, "My Battle with Anorexia and Schizophrenia," *Canadian Woman Studies*, vol. 24, no. 1, fall 2004, pp. 49–51. Copyright © 2004 *Canadian Woman Studies*. Reproduced by permission of the publisher and the author.

ganized speech and thinking, social isolation, false beliefs, hallucinations, and hearing voices. It is *not* multiple personalities. Schizophrenia is a chemical imbalance. It is a medical problem.

As a woman, I experienced the symptoms a little differently. And from what I've studied and seen, every individual's experience with schizophrenia is different. My experience was so different from the norm, that doctors thought I was only suffering from anorexia. I also had symptoms of anorexia.

A Surprising Diagnosis

I went to the Counseling and Development Centre at York University so I could talk to someone about my thinking difficulties. The counselor told me that she would speak to the director of the Centre for advice on where to send me to treat my thought disorder, or schizophrenia. A few days later, when I came back, she said, "We think you should go to the eating disorder clinic at the Toronto General Hospital."

"But I don't want to get involved with any eating disorder program."

"Maybe you should talk to the psychiatrist on campus and see where she thinks you should go."

Really Healthy?

That's what I did. I walked into her office. She didn't notice that I had a problem—and I was glad about that. So, she was friendly at first. I thought people would despise me if they knew about my thinking problems, such as my fragmentation of ideas. I felt that all the information and ideas in my head were in parts that couldn't connect. I remember laying in bed at night and trying to connect an abundance of ideas but I couldn't do it no matter how hard I tried.

The psychiatrist thought I was normal, though. She was concerned about my inability to see anything because I didn't have my glasses with me. My blindness prevented her from seeing my thinking problem. She said I could see a doctor at the local hospital about joining a group for "healthy" people. I didn't talk to her about my thinking problems at all. She couldn't focus on more than one thing at a time.

Wanting to Be Different

I wandered off to the hospital's psychiatry wing. There were lots of people I considered weird. Some were talking loud, dressed in rags—old shirts, socks under skirts, messy hair and lots of smudged makeup—red and black. But I wasn't so different. Just like with anorexia, always comparing myself to other anorexics. I wondered if I was as sick as the people in the ward. When the psychiatrist asked me to come to her office, I was incoherent. I was talking about irrelevant things without connecting ideas. Originally, I wanted to talk about my thinking problems, but I didn't have to. The doctor nodded at everything I said, and she said, "You must be doing badly in school."

"Not really," I defended myself. I wanted to be smart but also different—a symptom of anorexia.

The next day I went back to the psychiatrist at the university and she talked to the psychiatrist at the hospital. The York [University] psychiatrist recommended that I go on antipsychotic drugs because the other doctor told her I had a thought disorder. She recommended me to the Centre for Addiction and Mental Health where I was put on medication. The doctor who gave me the prescription looked at me as though I was stupid. Most people with schizophrenia already feel poorly about themselves and they are very sensitive to what others think of them whether or not their teachers, strangers, or family are critical of them.

A Change in Surroundings

That summer before I was introduced to the possibility of taking medication. I went to Israel for a couple of months and my thinking got better there, without any meds. Of course, I still had delusions. I thought the people who ran the Jewish philosophy and science program I was in didn't want me to eat and I didn't eat. But my concentration and memory did improve.

I played Chinese checkers with a friend and that helped to improve my thought processes. Working on my thinking to get it better was a requirement to improve.

When I got back, I was very thin and depressed. I was admitted into the hospital where I recovered. There was no shame of being in a psychiatric hospital. My friends came to visit me and I was happy. My appetite came back. No more delusions or hallucinations. I did well for two years.

Slipping into Psychosis

Strangely, my thought disorder was caused by my eating disorder but I needed a specialist in schizophrenia because my eating disorder had turned into psychosis. That time, my mother took me to the Centre for Addiction and Mental Health because I thought that the reason I was so thin was because I had AIDS from that professor. But my thinness from AIDS was an excuse. I was really anorexic and I was ready to harm this prof because I blamed everything on her. This seemed obvious when I got off my meds. I was put on Risperidone, an antipsychotic drug.

The staff at the Clarke cared and did not demean me. I was there three months. At first, the staff did not think I was smart because my thinking was horrible. By the end, they encouraged me to return to university, and of course I trusted them.

A Complicated Condition

Unfortunately my weight went up to 154 lbs from a measly 110 as a result of the drug. This upset me greatly. My biggest fear was of becoming huge and I was huge. I went off my meds after two years of taking them. I didn't even know what my diagnosis was because I was diagnosed with both depression and schizophrenia and later with schizophrenia caused by anorexia. Sure enough, the diagnosis straightened itself out.

Many times doctors find it difficult to diagnose because depression, manic depression, and schizophrenia can be so similar. There may be psychosis in depression and manic depression usually has psychosis. I had a psychotic relapse three weeks after going off meds. I was devastated. I didn't want to go back on meds. I was nauseous until I went back on medication. I was nauseous because my body was being controlled by my old eating problem. That's one major symptom of schizophrenia—the body being controlled by stranger sensations that still affect the individual. But as a woman, my poor body image affected me in the most extreme way. It was making me acutely ill. You see, thinking I had AIDS was not to blame. My eating disorder was controlling my body. It was not a withdrawal symptom either. My physical problem started weeks after stopping the meds.

A Problem Patient

During the first episode of psychosis, doctors were confused. Was it anorexia or schizophrenia? As a woman, I was complicated. I don't mean to say that women are complicated. What I mean is the psychiatric system has difficulties catering to women because more women have depression and not schizophrenia.

My thinking was so poor that I couldn't express what I was experiencing. For example, I couldn't tell the doctors that thoughts and ideas were being put into my head by faculty and students at the university. This is a core symptom of schizophrenia. The doctors only saw that I was thin and disorganized. They found it hard to diagnose me because of that. But they did their best.

Harmful Delusions

My parents called the hospital once they noticed I wasn't eating or drinking. The hospital thought my inability to eat had something to do with the anorexia and it did. I was determined to become grossly thin. I was certified (held against my will) after a few visits to emergency where I went willingly so I could determine whether or not I had the AIDS virus. All these delusions seemed true to me—the newspapers were telling me I had AIDS and I believed them. But on the other hand I was happy that I was losing weight. And the eating disorder took over the AIDS delusion. I'm not suggesting that the AIDS delusion was not important, but a big part of me was indeed anorexic. I didn't eat on purpose to look emaciated. I was afraid of becoming fat again. I thought that my weight was making me important and I thought I was special to everyone in the hospital. I thought they were talking about my anorexia and sending messages through the TV, the newspapers, and talking.

Professional Success

A year later, I graduated from York University. Then I was dysfunctional for a year until I got connected with the Work Adjustment Program at the Centre for Addiction and Mental Health. I was placed in the Public Affairs Unit. Christa Haanstra, the director of Public Affairs wanted me to write articles. The first one I wrote was an extensive profile of the Public Affairs staff and it was published!

From there, I succeeded. I had a wonderful portfolio and I got a lot of positive attention from staff and clients of the Centre. Everyone enjoys my articles.

The Centre for Addiction and Mental Health is a great hospital. I would not be in the Corporate Communications program without them. They gave me the opportunity to succeed. Thank you Work Adjustment program. Thank you Christa.

A New Way of Life

I don't like being on medication still, but I am being coerced to take it. I get Modecate [antipsychotic drug] injections once a month. Even though the Work Adjustment helped me, meds help me too and I don't have much of a choice (even if I wasn't forced) to take them. I am told that if I don't come in for my injections I'll get sick again, so I go.

I've fought my mental health issues for many years, and I want to get to a point where I don't fight my medication. Why should I? At the Centre for Addiction and Mental Health the patients come first and not ignorance. And the Centre knows what's best for me even though they are coercing me to take medication. Look, I'm married to a great guy, I have a degree in Women Studies from York University, and I have an excellent relationship with my parents.

A Diverse Disease

People with schizophrenia can recover and do well if they stick to their meds!

Everyone experiences something different with schizophrenia. The doctors tell me it is rare to have schizophrenia after an eating disorder. As a woman, my eating disorder provoked my psychotic episode. Others hear voices or think they are King David or someone else very important. But there are common symptoms that both men and women have such as visual hallucinations, disorganized speech and thought processes, fragmentation, social isolation, and poor concentration and memory. Women have to educate the system about their personal needs and experiences. Everyone has a different story.

CHAPTER 2

Family Connections

A Mother's and Daughter's Diaries

Linda M. Rio and Tara M. Rio

Psychologists, psychiatrists, and others who work with patients with eating disorders have long realized that treating an eating disorder can involve working with whole families, who try to understand the triggers for the disease and to develop mechanisms for coping and healing.

Tara Rio developed anorexia and bulimia as a teenager. This excerpt from The Anorexia Diaries, *a book Tara co-wrote with her mother, Linda, includes passages from both Tara's and Linda's diaries during one month in the fall of Tara's junior year in high school, when symptoms of her disease grew more pronounced and troubling. Tara, who acknowledges suffering from deep depression during this time, frankly discusses her aversion to having her mom get involved with treatments. Meanwhile, Linda, who had up until this point turned a blind eye to Tara's disordered eating, confronts her own denial, fear, and frustration with her daughter's illness.*

In addition to excerpts from Tara's and Linda's diaries, this selection also includes an introductory passage, written by Tara, as well as commentaries by both mother and daughter, as they reflect on the diary entries more than a decade after they were originally written.

Linda M. Rio is a clinical psychologist working primarily with child and adolescent survivors of trauma and violence. Tara M. Rio is now the mother of two daughters, and she works as a public relations executive with a major corporation.

One of the most dangerous aspects of my eating disorder was the overwhelming need to keep my disease a secret. At first I was in denial. I believed that I had control over what I ate and how many times I threw up. I thought I could stop at any time. There came a point, though, when I realized that I couldn't control my fast spiral downhill. But even then I wasn't ready to give up my coping mechanism. I became paranoid that someone would find out and make me stop. Having to hide this secret from the people I cared about was one of the most painful parts of the disease. I wanted to reach out to my mom for help, but I was afraid she wouldn't respond and I would end up more wounded. I was also consumed with anger, which acted as a solid wall blocking me from connecting with her.

When my parents did find out about my illness, I felt a mixture of trepidation and relief. I was scared that they would make me stop and I would get fat and become more depressed. But I was also relieved that my mom took the matter so seriously. It showed me that she was concerned about my well-being and committed to helping me feel better.

I also wanted to share this vital part of my life with Mitch [Tara's boyfriend]. I wanted him to know how much pain I was in. I wanted him to nurture me and take that pain away. Ultimately, I wanted Mitch to save me from myself. But when I gently hinted about my "bad eating habits," he reacted angrily. He was understandably concerned about my health and didn't know how to help me. My relationship with him served as validation that I was desired and worthy of love, which is why the thought of it ending drove me to the brink of my depression.

During this time, I remember feeling torn between wanting to nurture my swimming talent and wanting to die rather than be seen in a swimsuit. I battled with this inner dilemma until my junior year of high school, when my self-loathing won out and I quit the swim team just after being named captain of the varsity team. The idea of even more people watching me compete with this new status drove me to give up the one thing I felt I did well. I went from a lifestyle where I burned an enormous amount of calories through my daily workouts to a more sedentary one. This drastic shift created a deeper sense of paranoia about weight gain and more free time to feel it. The adrenaline was noticeably absent from my life, leading me to find a new way to achieve the rush I used to feel from swimming.

Tara's Diary

9/4/89

Last night was a disaster. I had dinner with mom and dad. I ate a small meal then went into the bathroom and threw it up like normal. They assumed I kept it down and I went out and watched a movie with them. When I was getting ready for bed my mom came in to say goodnight, but first she went into the bathroom and found my dinner in the toilet. I guess it didn't flush all the way down. She came into my room and asked if I had vomited. I had a feeling she must have known, so I just smiled and said, yeah mom a little, it's no big deal. I'll never forget the look on her face. It showed anger, pain and worst of all disappointment.

Once again she dragged me in to tell my dad. This time she wasn't so nonchalant. My mom told me she was finding me some help. I guess I'm lucky to have parents that care as much as they do, although right now I wish they didn't care so much.

9/8/89

Yesterday I went to see an eating disorders specialist up in Santa Barbara. It was pretty cool because I didn't have to go to school. But mom had to miss work and it seemed like she was really mad at me all day.

The doctor diagnosed me with [anorexia and bulimia]. Basically, I eat very little food and whatever I do eat I throw up. The doctor kind of scared me. He said that this is the most dangerous kind of eating disorder because I'm not letting my body get any nutrients whatsoever. When he examined me he said that my throat was red and burned. He said my teeth were beginning to lose their enamel from the vomiting. He did an EKG (I think) and said that my heart was not functioning like it was supposed to. He said the constant throwing up was straining my heart—but I think he's making that up. How could throwing up affect your heart? He also said I had gastrointestinal-something or other. I think he was just trying to scare me . . . and it may have worked.

9/22/89

My mom just called from work. She said she made me another appointment with the doctor in Santa Barbara that specializes in "this sort of thing." She can't even bring herself to say it she's so disappointed. I know she's embarrassed too. What a bitch. I'm the one in pain and all she can think about is what effect this will have on her reputation in the community.

I really don't see why I need to go to any doctor anymore anyway. There isn't anything wrong with me. I need to do what I am doing in order to keep in shape. I wish everyone would just leave me alone. Yesterday I told Kyla and Jill about what I have been doing. I thought they would understand. We always diet together and talk about all the parts of our body that we would like to change. Instead of being supportive of me they completely went over the deep end. They yelled at me and told me I was going to hurt my body by what I was doing. I don't know what they are talking about. I am just trying an extreme diet. I have to diet like this. If I don't, Mitch won't want to go out with me anymore. All guys like thin girls. So I don't care what everyone is saying—I know I'm doing what I have to for myself.

Linda's Diary

September 4, 1989

I cannot believe what just happened tonight. Last week Tara basically told me that she has been making herself throw up. I've been so upset by this that I haven't even been able to write. I made her tell her dad, foolishly thinking he would scare her out of doing this anymore. (It used to work when she was a child. She has always been so frightened of his loud, booming voice.) Unfortunately, Lou didn't exactly provide her with the scolding I was hoping for. He's not even taking this seriously. He says this is a phase that she will grow out of. This last week I've been hanging on to this, trying so hard to believe it, even though I know better. And now tonight has confirmed all my fears.

We ate dinner as a family, like we normally do on Sundays. After dinner Tara excused herself (after eating very little). I had this feeling in my gut. I walked down the hallway and stopped outside the bathroom door and heard her vomiting. I went back out to watch TV and Tara came out to watch with us. I didn't say anything to anyone. I was just sitting there in shock. I wasn't sure how to handle it or if what I thought I heard was real. Then I went to the bathroom before I said goodnight to her and I saw it. Right there in the bottom of the toilet were little pieces of vomit that hadn't flushed all the way. This is real now. I can't ignore it.

Later—

I'm not going to waste any time in getting her (us!) help. I can't sleep again. Oh my god! I don't think I will ever forget. I knew it. I just knew it. Damn. I knew it! That damn kid is sick—really sick. Louie doesn't see how freaking scary this is. I don't know if I handled it right. I think I did. I hope I did! Oh god, oh god, oh god grant me some wisdom. I really need wisdom!

September 8, 1989

I don't think I will ever forget yesterday's doctor's office. The office was nicely furnished, but not elaborate. I liked the plants in his office. Tara and I sat there listening to him behind his big desk tell us that Tara was indeed sick. This shouldn't have been surprising to me, but it was.

I came home and told Lou everything the doctor said and it was difficult for him to hear. The doctor confirmed her diagnosis of [anorexia and bulimia]. I could feel the anger in my body when he was talking. I was so tense, my stomach hurt. Wow, that is funny, huh ... a tense stomach while finding out your daughter has an eating disorder! Ironic?? Part of me was watching and listening from outside myself, up in the corner of the room or something (disassociation?). I guess I was dissociating from myself because it was so difficult to be there, yet I knew I was doing the right thing by having her there. A part of me could not help being clinical, a therapist, yet I felt so incredibly stupid for being there! I know I selfishly wanted the doctor to see me as a fellow professional, yet I know he could not do that. He had to treat me, us, just like anyone else, because we are.

September 23, 1989

Things are busy, scary. I feel like I'm the only one trying to help Tara get better. Her father isn't helping at all. He just hides at work most of the time. Why is it that mothers are always left to clean up all the messes? Even the doctors and insurance companies aren't helping me. And God knows Tara is not helping herself get better. Why won't she just try? It's like she doesn't care whether she lives or dies. . . .

Looking Back

Tara

I believe the first time I tried to vomit, I was simply experimenting with an unhealthy habit. Like sneaking a puff off my friend's cigarette or sipping the alcohol from my parents' liquor cabinet, my natural, experimental teenage rebellion was in full force. So I sometimes wonder why I didn't become an alcoholic or a drug addict. All I know for sure is that from the moment I hung my head over the toilet and felt the rush of adrenaline reach my temples, I knew I was in love. Like a heroin addict longing for the next hit, I would sit in class and daydream about when I would get the next opportunity to vomit. I craved the high it gave me, and I was obsessed with planning the ways I would elevate that high. My new obsession eased my anxiety and anger while keeping me thin. It seemed like the perfect coping mechanism.

Of course, it wasn't long before this "coping mechanism" began to take control of my life. In my weekly sessions with my psychologist, we worked on dealing with the emotions behind my disordered eating and finding alternative, healthy coping strategies. Yet despite this, I couldn't seem to truly get better. I began to wonder if I would even make it through my teen years. I was keenly aware of my mortality. I thought about dying almost every day. Dreading the idea of waking in the morning, I used to lie in bed and beg God to take me in the middle of the night. I stopped dreaming about the future because I was certain my future was bleak. I felt like I had ruined my life and there was no way to get it back on track. Ironically, this complacency may have helped ease some of the anxiety I was experiencing. I had become so depressed that I stopped caring about getting into college, maintaining a perfect persona, or pleasing my parents.

At this time, I went into a severe depression. I didn't leave my bed for 2 days. I didn't eat or drink anything. I got up only to go to the bathroom. I could see the look of disgust in my parents' eyes. I think they just thought I was being a lazy teenager. At my lowest point, I cut my wrists with a piece of glass from the picture frame that held Mitch's picture.

I was at a point that night where I didn't really want to die . . . I don't think. I simply wanted to feel physical pain. The pain I felt in my heart was too severe. I had to release it somehow, and throwing up was no longer enough. Cutting my wrists was yet another way to divert the focus away from feeling the real pain inside. Watching the blood rise to the surface of my skin gave me the high that throwing up used to give me. My parents walked in my room and saw me lying in my bed stoically staring at my wrists. I looked up at them with puffy, red eyes and said, "I'm ready, I'll go to the hospital."

Admitting that I needed help seemed like admitting utter failure. Yet I now realize that it actually took an enormous amount of courage to admit that I could not deal with my problems by myself. And it took an equal amount of courage for my parents to accept and seek to understand my illness. Had my parents ignored my disorder (because of their own denial issues or otherwise), I am certain I would not be here today. In addition, had they not been so active in my recovery, I think the healing process would have taken much longer.

Linda

As I reflect upon the days that followed my eyes finally opening to Tara's illness, I remember first shock, then going completely into task mode. Once I "got it," I knew my husband and I had to act fast. I spent a lot of time on the telephone interviewing therapists and doctors. I knew Tara's behavior was serious. I had no idea at the time how serious it had already become, however.

When I asked Tara how many times she had forced herself to vomit, she said just a few. She lied. I wanted to believe her, but I knew even a few was too much. I knew from my limited training on eating disorders that this had to be treated, not ignored. I also knew that lying was a part of the illness, and I felt devastated to realize my own daughter would lie to me. I felt strong and weak at the same time. I felt strong in my conviction to get help; I felt weak and stupid for not acknowledging it sooner. The moment I discovered she cut herself with glass, I knew we would need to hospitalize her. I had no doubts then.

A Grandmother's Gift

Laura Collins

Many times, the parents of a teenager with an eating disorder become essential members of the treatment team whose job it is to monitor progress, enforce treatments, and impose discipline when necessary. At a time when parent–child relationships are already stressed by illness and confusion, these types of treatments, although often effective, can further compromise tense relationships.

In this essay, Laura Collins, whose daughter Olympia developed anorexia at age fourteen, discusses the unique and potentially essential role of grandparents in the process of healing teens with eating disorders. Collins's mother-in-law, Rose, initially saw Olympia's illness as a rejection of family, food, and self—all the things Rose valued. But as Olympia's parents became increasingly involved in an effective but stressful treatment program, Rose discovered that she had her own role to play in Olympia's recovery—as a source of comfort food, and of comfort. Collins also acknowledges her own indebtedness to Rose, who helped Collins overcome her own loneliness and self-doubts during Olympia's treatment.

Laura Collins is a writer and activist dedicated to involving parents in the treatment of their children's eating disorders. She has written extensively about the "Maudsley treatment" she describes in this article and is the author of Eating with Your Anorexic.

Olympia was my mother-in-law's first granddaughter. The mother of two boys, Rose was delighted to have a young girl to bring to teas, buy dresses for and to whom she could

Laura Collins, "Rose's Gift," *Women's League Outlook*, vol. 176, Fall 2005, pp. 38–40. Copyright © 2005 Women's League for Conservative Judaism. Reproduced by permission.

pass down family traditions. The two of them had a special relationship in which I, mother and daughter-in-law, played only a supporting role.

In 2002, when she was 14, Olympia became anorexic. Our job as parents was clear. We were busy interviewing doctors, psychiatrists and therapists. We drove hours for appointments and screenings. We read books, made phone calls and consulted experts.

As frontline caregivers, we were constantly active. Rose, on the other hand, felt helpless. Unable to give her good news, we rarely called her. Unable to enjoy visits, we stopped visiting. For parents, a child's eating disorder comes without a guidebook; for grandparents, there is no guidance at all.

Confused and Helpless

Rose wondered if something she had done or said had hurt Olympia. She worried that she had missed some sign and neglected to warn us. When she did see her beloved granddaughter, Rose was frightened by the shrinking body and sunken eyes and unsure whether to talk about it or what to say.

"Why is she doing this? Doesn't she know how beautiful she is?" she finally asked me.

We were just as confused. We felt guilty, frightened and sometimes angry. It took time for my husband and me to accept the diagnosis, to determine a direction of care, and to recognize that the illness would not simply—or quickly—go away. Explaining this to everyone who loved Olympia was painful and exhausting.

"No One Saw It Coming"

As it is with many children afflicted with eating disorders, no one saw it coming. We were a loving family and our daughter was accomplished and well-adjusted. We were financially comfortable, had excellent insurance and health care and we were actively involved in our local Jewish congregation as well as in the larger community.

Olympia appeared to be destined for great things. Rose, like most grandmothers, spoke proudly of her grades, artwork, social grace, and maturity.

Now all Rose could do was worry and pray. She supported us as we took one approach and then another. She listened when we called to cry, to rant or to share any bit of good news. Notably, throughout our initial struggles and missteps, there was no meddling, no second-guessing, no recriminations. At a time when many families turn against each other, my mother-in-law simply kept asking: "What can I do?"

For a few months, our painful answer was "Nothing, thank you." The therapists we consulted told us not to talk about food nor monitor Olympia's intake. We drove her to appointments and paid the bills and watched as her health declined. We received contradictory and frightening advice. We were not consulted or updated by Olympia's caregivers. It was a horrible time.

A New Approach

One day, my husband read about an innovative approach to anorexia care used in Great Britain since the 1980s called the "Maudsley approach." We eagerly devoured information about the therapists there who put control of what and when to eat into the hands of the parents of eating disordered adolescents.

"Food is medicine" these doctors said. We learned that many of the cognitive and physical symptoms of anorexia are a result of the starvation itself. This approach assumes the potentially deadly disease is controlling the child. Parents are taught to protect the child lovingly from starvation as a team with the therapist and other caregivers.

The next day, we stopped watching Olympia starve. The therapist fired us. We found a new doctor and new professional support. From that day on we served full meals, and firmly instructed her to eat them. We supported her through every painful bite but we did not bargain, compromise or argue.

A Way to Help

My mother-in-law knew a good thing when she saw it. Watching a child starve went against everything Rose believed in. Feeding people, and feeding them well, is one of Rose's best skills.

My mother-in-law's kugels, hamentaschen, macaroni and cheese casseroles, pesto sauces, hallah, and nut breads arrived by the bagful, neatly labeled, lovingly packaged. Instead of cutting calories, she used her extensive nutritional knowledge to add calories. She sent recipes, clipped articles and delivered food.

At Grandma's, unlike at home, food preparation and full meals have never been an afterthought. Rose does not believe in TV dinners and would not think of skipping a meal. Her refrigerator, freezer, and pantry could get us through a month-long lockdown if necessary. She has a set of dishes for every eventuality, a utensil for every use, an extra oven. "Fast food" means defrosting a full meal of wholesome, tasty leftovers.

Rose knows food. She knows how to cook, what to cook and how much to cook. When our household had to learn to serve three square meals and two high-calorie snacks seven days a week, it was a perfect job for Super Grandma.

Signs of Improvement

Rose, relieved finally to have something to do, demonstrated her openness to learning more about anorexia. We shared with her as we learned. She learned to treat Olympia and the disease as separate entities. She stood in a common front with us against the illness, but not against Olympia. She refrained from calling foods good or bad. She offered the loving and unconditional support she always had, and doubled it.

Although Olympia initially cried after every meal, within a week she was stronger. In a few months of consistent and full nutrition, her lost weight was regained. Along with improvement in her physical health, her anxiety and irrational urges to restrict food abated. After six months she was eating on her own, with emotional support and supervision. A year later she was making her own choices, healthily, and leading a normal life. She was not hospitalized, and she did not miss a day of school.

A Safe Place

As Olympia healed, Rose cheered along with us. Once we had a plan in place, she eagerly became an important part of our treatment team. As a grandmother, Rose's role was to be an additional layer of support. Her house was a safe haven away from home. It was the first place Olympia could eat without our supervision. It was the first place she could sleep overnight since her illness began.

With Rose, Olympia was not required to talk about her feelings. While we were the disciplinarians, Rose could be an understanding and comforting adult. At Rose's house, Olympia was free from our lectures on eating disorders.

In addition to supporting Olympia, Rose supported me. The isolation of having a sick child is exacerbated with a mental disorder. We told few of our acquaintances and only a small number of friends. My loneliness was debilitating. Rose was there to listen, to encourage and to help me keep perspective. It was rare that a day went by without a check-in phone call, a card or a gift. When I doubted myself, she was a fierce defender. When I ranted, she agreed. When I was optimistic, she ran with that attitude, as well.

A Unique Role

My mother-in-law and I, we would both admit, had not been instant best friends. But instant relationships are overrated. A family that sees illness and tragedy can react with distrust and anger or with unity and increased respect. Ours came together. I can never repay my mother-in-law for her unique role in Olympia's recovery. I was humbled and honored to receive the generosity of spirit she gave us and our children in a difficult time. This closeness only makes the good times sweeter.

Eating disorders can tear a family apart, but grandparents can serve an important role. Far from helpless, they are in a unique position to support both the parents and the child.

Thank you, Rose. May I be as good a mother-in-law and grandmother in my time as you are now. I am in your debt always.

Stopping the Cycle

Anne Burt

Neither Anne Burt nor anyone in her family has ever been diagnosed with an eating disorder. But the uncomfortable relationship in her family among food, fat, and body image resembles the kind of obsessive thinking characteristic of those with more serious eating disorders.

Burt's own pregnancy—and the reactions of her doctors, her family, and even herself to her rapid weight gain—initiated her reflections on her family's deep-seated ambivalence toward food and weight gain. Burt recalls her mother's self-deprivation and cutting remarks about food, and body shape and chafes at her father's well-meaning but hurtful comments about her own pregnant body and, later, her infant daughter's pleasing plumpness. Finally recognizing the depth of her own feelings of fear, guilt, and self-loathing with regard to weight gain, Burt vows not to pass on those same feelings to her own daughter. Burt's essay effectively illustrates the extent to which disordered thinking about food and wellness has become socially acceptable in our culture.

Anne Burt is a writer whose articles have appeared in Working Mother, The Christian Science Monitor, *and on National Public Radio. She is also the editor of the anthology* My Father Married Your Mother: Dispatches from the Blended Family *and a coeditor of the collection* About Face: 25 Women Look in the Mirror and Write About What They See.

I wanted it to be my mother's problem.

She was the one obsessed with weight. She was the one who hated her thighs. She cooked our meals, making nothing

Anne Burt, "Fat Like Mommy," Salon.com, December 5, 2000. This article first appeared in Salon.com, at http://www.salon.com. An online version remains in the Salon archives. Reprinted with permission.

but salad for herself, then hovered over the kitchen sink sucking shreds of chicken meat off the bones we left behind because she was so hungry. Not me, I always declared. I have a positive sense of self. My body is my home.

A New Perspective

Then my body became somebody else's home. Within 10 weeks after my pea-size fetus moved in, that home gained 15 pounds.

"Your mother only gained 15 pounds throughout her entire pregnancy with you," said my dad.

"Well, she also smoked throughout her entire pregnancy with me," I answered, in a weak attempt to hide how fat and inadequate I felt. After I hung up the phone, I went to my kitchen and made a pot of macaroni and cheese. It was July. I was so hot and so nauseated that all I could do was lie on the sofa in front of the air conditioner or eat pasta. Sometimes, when I did both at the same time, I counted it as exercise.

Cold Advice

"You're gaining too much weight," my first obstetrician declared from behind his enormous desk. He was looking at my chart, not at me. He held the manila file with the records of my pregnancy thus far. His fingers were thick and stained with the unnatural caramel color that comes from regular sessions at a tanning salon.

"What do you think I should do about it?" I asked him, prepared to hear about nutritionists, prenatal exercise programs and salad. He tapped his fingers on the desk. I couldn't imagine this man reaching inside me to help pull out my child.

"Eat less," he said, still looking at my chart.

At that moment, I knew I was leaving his practice. What if I hadn't read all those books about pregnancy and I had interpreted "eat less" to mean "diet"? I could seriously harm my baby by following his idiotic advice. He droned on, spewing some incomprehensible crap about pregnant pioneers in covered wagons bouncing merrily over the prairies and how modern women worry too much. ("Although you're a Jew, right?" he asked. When I answered yes, he said, "Me too. Our ancestors didn't know from covered wagons.")

To my recollection, lots of those carefree pioneers died en route to the West. I asked the receptionist to make copies of that chart of mine before I left.

But the doctor's words had left an indelible impression. I was gaining too much weight. Suddenly, all my self-assurance went right out the window. Every pregnancy-related pound I added made me sweat in fear of a lifetime of fat.

"Let's see what the damage is," the nurse said each time I stepped on the scale at my new OB's office. I would fume at her choice of words—and yet I said nothing, because underneath my righteous anger I had the guilt-ridden, self-hating certainty that weight gain *was* damage. I was out of control. I was bad.

Out of Control

Meanwhile, my mother had started lifting weights and eating a high-protein diet during my pregnancy. She emerged from her regimen looking small and hard, and expressed delight that my father, too, was lifting weights so that by contrast, she looked even smaller. I was big. I loved my pregnant belly, loved its undulations as the baby grew legs and put them to use. I did not love my pregnant thighs, hands, upper arms and chins (I had three by my count). By the final month, I kept my eyes closed when I stepped onto the scale at the doctor's office. After I had gained 45 pounds of pregnancy weight, I stopped counting.

I felt guilty and small-minded for worrying about fat. I was nurturing a child, I told myself: My body had donated its services to the protection of this brand-new human. But fat was fat. And to see my mother slimmer by the day made me feel more slovenly, even less maternal. How could I take care of a baby when I couldn't even take care of myself? My mother was in control. I was out of control.

Consumed by Worry

My daughter was born Feb. 5. She weighed 6 pounds, 2 ounces—the exact amount that both my sister and I had weighed when we were born. She was such a tiny thing, too little for most of the newborn-size clothing we had waiting for her. But she started eating, and she started growing. And growing. I never understood the expression "to blossom" so well before. Blossom is exactly what she did. I'm still amazed that simply by sucking on my breasts, this person grew round and bright and glorious.

"She's a fatty!" said my dad when he saw her at 4 months old.

"She's not too fat! She's perfect!" I snarled at him.

"I didn't say she was too fat. I meant it in a good way," he muttered. Well, maybe, I thought, but as far as I was concerned, there could be no such thing as being fat in a good way. Not when I recalled my father running five miles every day; my mother baking tofu croutons with garlic powder to add protein to her salad; my sister traveling to her weekly Weight Watchers weigh-ins. How had I failed to notice that my mother's problem with consumption had consumed my family? And how could I think I had escaped?

Instilling the Fear

I remember twirling in front of a mirror in a dressing room with my mother when I was in high school, admiring a skirt I'd decided to buy.

"I love it," I said.

"Oh, it's great," she responded. "It works miracles for your thighs."

All the enjoyment I had about the skirt drained right out of me. According to my mother, I had to dress to hide myself, not for fun. Shopping trips with Mom were anxiety festivals: Does it slim my rear? Camouflage my hips?

In my early 20s, I started wearing miniskirts in furious protest against years of cover-up. Take that, Mom, I said to my reflection in the mirror as I examined my exposed thighs. I didn't realize that my defiance was just another mask for the innate fear of fat that had taken root too deeply to be excised with a piece of clothing.

I spent so many years angry at my mother for insisting that I was too heavy because she felt that she was too heavy. Leave me out of it, I yelled silently at her in my head. Why do you care if I look fat or thin?

Burying the Past

Now I find myself dressing my daughter in adorable, colorful little things, laughing as she laughs up at me from her changing table, her bright blue eyes screaming pleasure—and I'm worried that her thighs look fat. She's still a tiny baby, and already I'm doing it to her, too.

Finally I understand the intense attachment that makes a mother see her own fragile self-image blown up bigger than life in her daughter's legs. I rub my hands over the velvet skin dimpling my baby's gorgeous knees. I don't want her to look in the mirror someday and see my fears when she looks at her body.

When my parents hold my daughter, I see no judgment in their eyes of her roly-poly arms and legs. Not even my father's "fatty" comment goes beneath the skin. They treat her with pure love. Fear of fat is part of my family's history; now it's my goal to keep it history. Can my daughter learn that food is pleasurable, that exercise is pleasurable, that clothes are pleasurable?

Can my mother and I keep our mothers' problem to ourselves?

CHAPTER 3

A Diverse Disease

Midlife Anorexia

Roxanne Patel

Anorexics often speak of the desire to gain control over one aspect of their lives as a motivating factor in developing a dangerous eating disorder. Many of these patients are teenagers, a group who often feel that many other areas of their lives are controlled by others—from teachers to parents—but that an eating disorder is something they can control.

In Roxanne Patel's profile of Barbara Daub, Daub acknowledges the desperate need for control as one impetus for her life-threatening anorexia. But Barbara Daub is no teenager. She first developed anorexia in her late forties. Happily married with a successful career and two children in college, Barbara found herself unable to cope with the loneliness, stress, and sadness of the empty nest. Feeling hopeless, she turned to something she discovered she was very good at—losing weight. Daub's story underscores that the "typical" victim of an eating disorder is not necessarily a young girl—indeed, eating disorders among older women are on the rise.

Roxanne Patel is a writer and editor whose articles have appeared in Self, Good Housekeeping, *and* Glamour. *She now writes full-time for* Philadelphia *magazine.*

She was obese. At least, that's what Barbara Daub thought when she looked in the mirror. It didn't matter that she weighed 100 pounds and stood five feet eight inches tall. What she saw was a blond linebacker. And there was only one thing to do about that: Lose more weight.

Back in the fall of 1997, Barbara's life had seemed full. She'd been married for 26 years to Matthew, a painter and an art professor. They had raised two children, who were studying for their own careers as a lawyer (her son) and an artist (her daughter). Barbara herself was the executive director of a nonprofit family services organization in Kutztown, Pennsylvania. She was fit and healthy. At a trim 125 pounds, she ate whatever she pleased without gaining weight. And she enjoyed food—especially pasta during annual trips to Italy with her husband.

Making a Change

But inside, Barbara was struggling. With the children gone, her house seemed empty. Her job was stressful. The realization that she'd be turning 50 in a few years "hit me hard," says Barbara, who decided she needed to make a change. So she went on a diet, losing five pounds in two weeks. Then, for good measure, she lost five more. "Other people have trouble losing weight, but I was good at it," Barbara recalls. "I felt like a success."

Before she knew it, Barbara was hooked—dangerously so. Ten times a day, she stepped on a scale, holding her breath until she read the number: 120 pounds. . . 119. . . 115.5. Every ounce seemed like a victory. Within a few months, she'd stopped eating meat; then she stopped eating everything but dinner—a salad with no-calorie dressing. By mid-1998, when Barbara had lost 15 pounds, her husband started to worry.

"I can't believe that's all you're eating," Matthew said one evening. "That can't be enough!"

But Barbara wouldn't listen—not that night, or the next, or the next, as Matthew went from pleading to yelling to angry silence across the dinner table. Instead, she became even more intent on her diet. "I was angry at him for trying to tell me what to do," she says now. "I thought he was just trying to make me fat."

A New Problem

Over the next 18 months, Barbara lost 15 more pounds, withering into a shell of herself—physically and emotionally. She worked long hours and ran four miles a day. She no longer met friends for lunch or dinner, no longer spent time drawing. She could not even enjoy her children's visits. "The only thing that gave me pleasure was losing weight," Barbara says.

In early 2001, she quit her job. She had been seeing a therapist for depression, and, after several months, let the doctor talk her into enrolling at the Renfrew Center, a leading eating disorders clinic in Philadelphia. Like other centers across the country, Renfrew is seeing more and more older patients suffering from anorexia and its sister disorder, bulimia. Nearly a quarter of the women who sought treatment at the clinic last year were between 30 and 65, a jump of one third over four years. "It's not something people acknowledged for a long time," says Holly Grishkat, a site director at Renfrew who created a program specifically for older patients.

Progress and Setbacks

Even at Renfrew, Barbara didn't think she was sick at first. But forced to talk about her life—and to eat every crumb on her plate five times a day—she started to understand that she was starving herself as a way to gain control of her life, to avoid thinking about her true anxieties. And she finally realized that she was anorexic. "I heard my story through other people," she says now, "and I knew I fit the pattern."

At the end of the four-week stay, Barbara had gained about ten pounds and felt she was on the way to recovery. But within a few months, she was back at Renfrew for another course of treatment. Again, Barbara came home hoping she'd be able to get well. She understood what she was supposed to do: Eat five times a day—in her case, seven proteins, four fats, 13 carbs, four fruits, and four vegetables. She continued her therapy and also saw a nutritionist, who weighed her weekly and reviewed what she ate.

But she hadn't really changed. Her counselors told her they would send her back to Renfrew if she dropped below a certain weight—which they wouldn't divulge. So she spent all day plotting: *How much do I have to eat to stay out of Renfrew but not actually gain anything?* Her evenings were spent in tense standoffs with her increasingly weary husband. Then, by late summer of 2002, they weren't even fighting. Matthew had already made it clear that it would take a miracle for their marriage to survive.

"I'd Lost Everything"

That was probably Barbara's lowest moment. She had stopped following her food guidelines and going to the nutritionist. "It wasn't working, so there seemed no point," she says. Her weight, which had been hovering around 111 pounds, quickly dropped to 100. Without food, she could hardly think straight; she became breathless and dizzy. And she burst into tears easily, barely able to fathom what her life had become. "I'd lost everything—my career, my friends, my hobbies, my marriage."

Barbara was also on the verge of a medical crisis. At the end of August, a friend took her back to Renfrew—and just in time. Years of starving herself had put a strain on her heart. She was severely dehydrated, and her heart rate was very low. The doctors put her on strict bed rest for ten days. It turned out to be the wake-up call Barbara needed. "I knew I couldn't rely on anyone else to take care of me when I went home," she says. "Even my husband might not be there. I had to get well—for myself."

This time, Barbara stayed at Renfrew for six weeks and gained 25 pounds, bringing her weight back up to 125 pounds. At home, she continued to eat nutritious meals and has maintained that weight since—nearly three years now.

Finding Hope

Not that it's always easy. Barbara is still in therapy. And she has to remind herself that the woman she sometimes sees in the mirror—the fat woman who needs to diet—exists only in her imagination.

But today, Barbara is healthy and happy: She and her husband are together, building a new house and planning their next trip to Italy. They sit down for meals without fighting and enjoy dinner with friends.

The biggest change, though, has been in Barbara's outlook. "I feel optimistic for the first time in years," she says.

Black Women Get Eating Disorders Too

Lisa, as told to Nell Bernstein

Fewer than one percent of women diagnosed with anorexia or bulimia are African American. So although Lisa, a young black woman, suffered from anorexia and bulimia throughout much of high school and college, her condition went undiagnosed for years. Because so few black girls develop eating disorders, her family, friends, and even medical professionals refused to see what was really happening to Lisa. Instead, she was accused of having diabetes, low self-esteem, sickle-cell anemia, or even a drug problem.

Faced with a shortage of support in her personal life, unable to find information for African Americans with eating disorders, and repeatedly dismissed by the medical establishment, Lisa had to rely on herself for her own difficult recovery. Lisa's story draws attention to the danger of stereotyping victims of eating disorders; had her illness been properly diagnosed by medical practitioners who could see past Lisa's skin color to her condition, she might not have suffered to such an extent.

Nell Bernstein's articles have appeared in Salon, Glamour, Marie Claire, Self, *and many other publications. She is also the author of* All Alone in the World: Children of the Incarcerated.

I stood in the bathroom of my college dormitory, my heart pounding against my ribs. For months, I'd been making myself throw up into a plastic bag hidden under my bed, then sneaking into the bathroom late at night to throw away the evidence.

I kept telling myself I had things under control. But now, I was coughing up blood and waking up each morning with a sore throat. How on earth had I gotten to this point?

Lisa, as told to Nell Bernstein, "'You Can't Be Anorexic—You're Black!'" *Marie Claire*, December 2004, pp. 121-122. Reproduced by permission of the author.

Looking Back

My eating disorder had been slowly taking over my life. When I was a senior in high school, I starved myself down to 70 pounds and still thought I was fat. When I started my freshman year in college, I had every single characteristic of someone with severe anorexia and bulimia—except one. "You can't be anorexic," friends told me, "You're black."

Being African-American was somehow supposed to disqualify me from this "white girl" disease. In truth, my race couldn't prevent me from getting an eating disorder, but it did prevent me from getting the help I desperately needed.

Family Issues

Growing up, I ate whatever I wanted and never worried about my weight. In school, I was involved in everything—sports, yearbook, student senate, cheerleading. But my life outside school was far from perfect. My parents had divorced when I was young, and I lived with my mom and saw my dad on Saturdays. As a kid, our visits seemed pretty normal, but when I entered puberty, my father began buying revealing clothes for me and talking about how my body was changing. I had the stereotypical "black butt," and he'd touch it and make comments about how it looked.

When I told my best friend what was going on, she told her mother, and her mother called the police. Social services showed up at my school and started asking me questions. I didn't want my father to find out, so I said it was all a mistake. But after another incident a few months later, I told my mother what my father was doing.

After that, instead of wanting to see me in tight clothes, he started calling me fat. It became a control thing—not that he really cared what size I was, but that he could dictate what I looked like. At dinner, he'd only allow me to eat a salad—no dressing. He bought me exercise equipment and low-fat cookbooks.

"Stop Trying to Act White"

I was 17 years old, 5'2″, and 98 pounds. My whole life, I'd thought of myself as thin. Suddenly, I felt uncomfortable in my body. I never really ate breakfast anyway, and I stopped eating lunch, too, but I still didn't feel small enough. So I stopped eating dinner and subsisted on my once-a-day snack—a yogurt or a cookie.

One day, after my weight had dropped to about 80 lbs., my mom walked into my room while I was getting dressed. Staring at my skeletal frame, she unleashed a torrent of angry words. "I don't know what you're doing, but knock it off," she said. "You're not a white girl. Stop trying to act white."

But I couldn't stop—I was trying so hard to please my father! "Lose another 10 pounds, and you'll look great," he'd say. After all his criticism, he was finally being nice—it felt good to earn his approval. Soon, I was going two or three days without eating at all. I felt dizzy. My hair started getting straggly. People began to notice. The funny thing is, all the black kids thought I was taking drugs. It never occurred to them that I was starving myself.

No One to Turn To

In school, my white friends swapped diet pills and plotted ways to lose weight. But outside of school, my black girl-friends laughed if I mentioned the word "diet." And, despite my ever-diminishing size, my mother and I never talked about my problem. It was hard—we'd always been able to talk about anything: sex, friendships, politics. But body image isn't something black women discuss. Even really big women say, "I love my body, I love my breasts." For the first time, my mother lacked the words to help me.

I starved myself for my whole senior year. Finally, I passed out during track practice and was rushed to the hospital. The first thing the doctor said was, "Diabetes is prevalent in black families. Does anyone in your family have diabetes?" Then they wanted to check for sickle-cell anemia! They were grasping for anything black-related that would cause me to lose weight. By then, I'd lost more than 20 pounds—but anorexia never even came up!

I Didn't Fit the Profile

After high school, I went to a predominantly white college. Concerned about my weight, the nurse at the health center referred me to a counselor. But she couldn't see past my skin color, either. "How do you feel around white girls?" she asked. "Do you feel you have to compete with them to date white guys?" She decided being black had left me with a self-esteem problem. We never talked about my anorexia.

Shortly afterward, I started making myself sick—if I ate one M&M, it was coming up. I had to get my teeth filled three times because of decay from stomach acid. At times, I truly thought I might die.

When I confided to a black girlfriend about my eating disorder, she laughed at me. "Are you stupid?" she said. "That's not for us." How could I explain that I didn't know how to stop? Whenever I looked up anorexia on the Internet, the same list of characteristics would pop up: Wealthy family. Overachiever. White. I searched through black-women's magazines, but eating disorders were never covered.

On My Own

In the middle of my confusion, I began dating a guy who was really supportive. He let me talk about my eating disorder—something no one else did. And he ate with me. It would take me an hour to finish a quarter of a sandwich, I'd cry my eyes out, but still he'd sit there. With his support, by my senior year of college, I started getting better.

It's true: Most women with eating disorders need professional help. But when my race became a roadblock to getting that support, I began the slow process of healing on my own.

One of the hardest parts was realizing that my father had wanted to tear me down—and did it so easily. Family should be about unconditional love. By manipulating that love, he'd set me down a path of self-hatred.

The moment that crystallized my struggle was the day I graduated from college. After the ceremony, my two little cousins ran up to me, wrapped their little arms around my robe, and said, "We're so proud of you." That's when I thought, *This* is what family is all about.

You're Not Alone

Today, I can't honestly say I eat three full meals every day, but I make sure I never go a whole day without eating. I try not to weigh myself too often, but the last time I got on the scale, I weighed 102. I may never love my body, but I'm at a point where I can accept it.

Anorexia is not a race issue. But I believe that if I were white, my eating disorder would have been handled differently by counselors, family, and friends. I hope that now, if a black woman skims through [articles] like I did, looking for advice, she will realize she's not alone.

The Color of Anorexia

Anna Whitehead

Anna Whitehead had always been relatively comfortable with her biracial identity. The daughter of a white mother and a black father, Whitehead thoughtfully and adeptly navigated her different identities. When she developed the "white girls' disease" of anorexia, however, her disorder sent Whitehead's sense of identity into question.

Even though Whitehead appears white, with blond hair and Caucasian facial features, she had always nurtured her African American heritage. Now, though, coping with a disease that overwhelmingly strikes white women, Whitehead was forced to grapple with whether she was, in fact, more white than black by virtue of the disease she had succumbed to. Anorexia can be a debilitating psychological disorder, for Whitehead it was doubly so, as developing the disease caused her to doubt her very sense of self.

Anna Whitehead is the publisher of the feminist zine With Heart in Mouth. *She lives in Washington, D.C.*

It's hard to deny that anorexia is a white girls' disease. This is not to say that *only* white people or *only* females develop eating disorders. But anorexics tend to be of the fair-skinned female persuasion. As a white girl, I know what it is like to consciously purge and deny myself food, take sleeping pills in lieu of eating, exercise furiously until I could feel the fat dripping from my brow in tiny beads of sweat. I also know what it is like to be black. I am white skinned, I am blonde haired, I listen to punk rock. I am white? But I have another side of me—one with a black father, one who attended family reunions with watermelons and fried chicken, one who has southern cousins with names like Bo and Punkin. I face my race every day. Sitting in my school cafeteria and watching the races and nationalities gradually divide into specific cliques I am often left grappling with the question: Where do I belong? When I sit with a certain group of friends who are entirely white, I notice. They may not, but I do. I have to make sure that I am "staying true to my race," whatever that is, because I am still black when I am at a punk show, and I am still white when I go to a black girls' conference.

Creating New Labels

It's hard. It sometimes feels like I am always struggling to catch up, because I wasn't born with that label to settle in to; for better or for worse, I have to create my own label. I haven't done it yet. I am still jumping between them, wondering when I can just be *me*.

Although the walls of hatred are crumbling a little more each year, we still live in an extremely racist society. It starts when you look at someone and see first the color of their skin. This is racism because it immediately establishes the wall of separation—this person is now identifiable as a person by their skin tone. So it is assumed that, should you both be of different races, you are already approaching life from two different angles, and perhaps, if you are white, you are coming from the angle of abuser. I don't want to be an abuser—or a victim, for that matter. The struggle to believe in myself as a woman or a teenager is great enough. Those things are real, and physical. Race is not. In all my attempts to be identified as what I am—not what I look like, which sexual organs I have, or how nappy my hair is—I became confused and lost sight of who I wanted to be. I concluded that I had been born into misinterpretation, and that I would only ever be accepted if I made it painfully obvious who it was I wanted to be accepted as. When someone is starving, it is very hard to ignore.

Just How White Am I?

So when I say that anorexia is a white girls' disease I mean that in the broadest sense. It is very hard always struggling to stay true to your "black roots" or "white heritage" or what have you, and then realizing you have a "white girls' disease."

What does that mean? Does that mean I copped out?

That I betrayed my black sisterhood and decided to become an All-American white girl? Or that I was never "black enough" to begin with? Was my anorexia just a disturbing reminder of how white I really am?

A Disease with Expectation

People, it seems, will always understand you by the way you look, and my eating disorder was no more direct than my race. I was open to interpretation (and misinterpretation) either as sickly and white, or confused and black.

Anorexia, and eating disorders in general, affect you physically and psychologically. In fact, it is your very psychology and socialization that causes it in the first place. A disease is a disease, but some diseases come tagged with certain expectations. When you disregard those expectations of an eating disorder, you are breaking the rules of race. What is a biracial girl to do when she finds out her lack of homogeneity even influences her disorders?

I can't, as much as I would like to, ignore my race, whatever that is. And I also don't want to hold myself to some statistical standard that says black folk are immune to self-starvation. But it is very hard, when you are so aware of the whiteness of your skin and the flatness of your nose, to disregard the color of your disorder.

Skinny Boy

Gary Grahl

In high school, Gary Grahl was on the fast track to success. He was an outstanding athlete, with baseball abilities that had caught the attention of big-league scouts. He was handsome, popular, and his future seemed bright—until an insidious voice in his head started convincing him to lose weight.

From normal athletic training, Grahl's exercise regimen quickly spun out of control, taking over his daily schedule and leaving him exhausted. He also began severely limiting his food intake to only a few hundred calories per day, not nearly enough to sustain his growing body or his intense level of physical activity.

In this selection, Grahl relates his experience as he checked into an eating disorder treatment facility. In conversation with his mother and his therapist, Grahl also includes the self-destructive messages of his inner voice, the one that convinced him to keep hurting himself and to refuse help at all costs. This selection reveals Grahl's various motivations for sustaining his disordered eating and exercise, thinking that is in many ways quite different from the types of thoughts reported by girls struggling with eating disorders. Eating disorders among young men and boys are on the rise; Grahl's story offers valuable insight into the reasons males might develop such disorders.

Gary Grahl recovered from his adolescent anorexia and is now a licensed school counselor. He serves as a resource person for the National Association of Anorexia Nervosa and Associated Disorders. He and his family live in Wisconsin.

The conversation starts out like most, superficial and dull. It's a game I don't care to play, although I'm quite good at it. Greta [my therapist] begins by commenting on the weather.

Mom reciprocates. There's a shallow attempt at humor from Greta, which fails but manages to extract some kind of fake chuckle from Mom and me. Then, the main course of questions is tossed on a plate in front of me.

"So, Gary," says Greta, getting comfortable in the chair. "How are you doing today?"

"Good."

"Are you ready for the long road ahead of you?"

Putting On a Happy Face

I shrug my shoulders and smile. I always smile in front of others. I smile when I'm happy. I smile when I'm sad. I smile when I'm upset. I smile when I'm embarrassed. Heck, I'd probably smile if an elephant was crushing my foot right now, all for . . . for . . . I don't know why. All I know is that I'm terrified of allowing anyone so much as a glimmer of the authentic me, whoever that is. At least smiles are safe.

"Gaa-ry!" says Mom. "Why don't you talk to Greta? This is the time to get help."

Help? Who needs help? You're doing just fine.

"I don't know what to say."

"Anything, talk about anything. Just talk. Lots of things are fair game," Mom pushes. "What about that one time you told me about being teased?"

Remember, back in elementary school, when he took great pleasure in squashing your—

Keep that jerk out of this, will you?

This silly mother issue isn't going to go disappear, you know.

I said shut up!

You're right. Talking will only cause more hurt feelings. I've trained you well.

The Boy in the Mirror

Guilt thrusts its sword into my side. My throat suddenly forgets how to talk. I heave a heavy sigh. Mom's is heavier, and includes a shaking head.

Greta gets wise in a hurry to the fact that she's not going to get anywhere with me right now. Greta and Mom head out the door for a brief powwow. My senses get a wake-up call from a washed-out gown that slaps me in the chest and falls to the examination table.

"Whoops!" says Greta, innocently. "Sorry, Gary, I thought you were looking. I'd like for you to change into this and knock when you're ready. I'll get your vitals and weight, and then we'll take a quick tour of the unit."

As soon as the door shuts, I immediately strip to my underwear and look into the full-length mirror on the wall. It's a familiar picture I gawk at dozens of times daily. I reach my arms high into the air as if I'm signaling a touchdown. I can feel my skin stretch tautly over twelve protruding ribs like thin plastic on a freezer-wrapped chicken. I turn to the side and bend over. The vertebrae on my backbone stick out sharply. The lower part of my spine is calloused black and blue from months of doing endless sit-ups on our linoleum bathroom floor. Pride momentarily rips through my conscience.

But it's just not good enough. You're still so flabby and soft. Your muscles aren't cut enough. Your legs aren't long enough. You're nothing but a cow.

The Monstrous Scale

Next to the mirror sits one of the most intimidating pieces of equipment ever invented by man: the scale. It's a tall steel monster with a heavy iron block that slides across a steel ruler, like the one the wrestlers use at school. Do I dare look this morning?

Of course. Your day will be unbearable if you don't.

I find my body automatically stepping up onto the cool metal platform, shifting the black block across the ruler to find—Aw man, what a rip! Is this thing broken? I do *not* weigh this much.

A knock comes at the door.

"Gary? Are you ready?"

I quickly hop off the scale, put my hospital gown back on, and sit up straight on the exam table. "Yeah."

Greta and mom come back in. A stethoscope hangs around Greta's neck, and she's carrying a clipboard. I feel uncomfortable. Greta takes my blood pressure, pulse, height, and weight. It's pathetic to her, a badge of courage to me: pulse, thirty-five beats per minute; height, five feet, eight inches; weight, 109 pounds—down a whole pound from yesterday. I shake my head like I'm really disappointed so Greta and Mom don't think I'm satisfied about the low weight.

Atta boy.

"Wow," says Greta, making notes on what I assume is my chart. "You are a sick young man. Given your activity level, your medium-to-large bone structure, and the fact that you're a growing teenage boy, you should be weighing in the neighborhood of 155 pounds, minimum."

She gives her head a little shake while ripping off the Velcro blood pressure cuff.

She steps out of the room so I can change into my civilian clothes, then returns with my mother.

A Typical Day

"I know we briefly touched on this last Friday during your initial evaluation," says Greta, "but take me again through a typical day for you."

Here's my chance to impress her once again.

"Well, I get up at 3:30 every morning—"

"In the morning?" cries Mom. "*Gaa*-ry! Why do you have to get up so early?"

"To exercise. I'm usually up anyhow."

Actually, I'm dead tired at that hour, but I've been forcing myself to rise earlier for months in order to accommodate my increased workout load.

"What do you do from there?" asks Greta.

"Well, I come downstairs and turn on the CNN News. After warm-up stretching I head outside for twenty fifty-yard sprints. Then it's back inside for fifteen miles on the exercise bike under heavy tension, five hundred sit-ups, three hundred push-ups, one hundred swings of my baseball bat both left and right handed, three hundred jumping jacks, and one hundred karate kicks with my right and left legs," I say, enthusiasm beginning to spill over in my tone. Thinking about my exercise routine gets my adrenaline surging. "Sometimes in the winter when the snow is really high, I like to add a three-mile run in our back field." I don't mention that I do this wearing heavy snow boots because I have to kick higher that way. "Finally, it's my cool-down stretching for about five minutes. Then it's off to breakfast."

"Ha! He barely eats enough to keep a bird alive," Mom mutters.

"How long have you kept this routine going?" asks Greta.

"About a year now."

Mom's hand frantically dives for her purse, then suddenly stops short as she realizes she can't light up in the hospital.

"Continue," says Greta.

An Obsessive Schedule

"Breakfast is usually three tablespoons of cereal with three tablespoons of skim milk. Then it's—"

"Ha!" exclaims Mom, her voice wheezy and heavy even though she's still working hard to maintain a pleasant smile. "It takes him nearly half an hour to eat that, too!"

I keep smiling, pretending that I'm not feeling perturbed about being interrupted.

"Then it's off to school. Lunch is usually a half peanut butter and jelly sandwich, an apple, and some skim milk. Sometimes, I eat just the apple. After school I come home and do another hour and a half of exercising, usually weight lifting and more bat swinging. For dinner I have some type of meat, potato product, and a vegetable—no more than three hundred to five hundred calories, depending on how much I exercised," I say, trying to be as thorough as possible. I'm secretly hoping to elicit some raised eyebrows and wide eyes. "Then it's off to do my homework or watch some TV, do my five-mile run, and hit the hay. A lot of nights, I like swinging my bat in my room before bed while I listen to some music."

"He broke his brother's stereo while swinging that thing," Mom interjects. Her smile is looking more and more forced. "And what about the time you took out your bedroom window, Gary?"

Actually, I forgot about that.

"Oh, and then there's his habit of walking around our pool table after meals. He thinks we don't know what he's doing, but we do."

The CIA would be impressed.

An Unrealistic Dream

Greta repositions in her chair, focusing on me. "Tell me again, why do you do so much exercising?"

"I'm in training to be a professional baseball player."

Mom is getting more steamed by the minute. Her lips are pursed together like she slurped some bad coffee. I have never seen her quite this agitated. The attention feels uncomfortable, but also good for some reason.

Why do you put your loving mother through this headache? You're embarrassing her.

"*Gaa*-ry! How the heck do you expect to play baseball with your weight so low? How do you know you're going to even wake up the next—"

"Pardon me for interrupting, Mrs. Grahl—"

Thank you. Someone put this poor woman on ice.

"—but I don't think it's going to do any good raising our voices in speculation right now," Greta says. "I do like that you're expressing your feelings. I think it helps Gary understand how much this affects you. However, I think it's important to use 'I' messages, like 'I'm feeling angry' or 'I don't like how your lifestyle is tearing you down.' We are responsible for our own feeling and actions."

Huh?

Mom and I look at each other, dumbfounded. That's not how we work.

I've trained you well.

I yawn. Another early wake-up call this morning with an intense workout has pacified my body. My eyelids feel like anchors.

The Truth Hurts

Greta gets to the point. "Gary, you're emaciated, but you see someone who's fat; you say you're training for baseball, but your exercise patterns are tearing your body apart; you're ravenously hungry, but deceive yourself into thinking your stomach is full—"

Wait a minute, how does she know that I—

"—You cannot be satisfied unless your muscles are crying out in pain and soreness; you will not allow yourself to enjoy the simple pleasures of life, but instead feel shame and guilt if success comes your way; you feel like you don't deserve good things in life—"

For a brief moment, Greta pokes her head through the window of my private world, causing me to duck and hide.

You will not listen to this hogwash! How dare this stranger tell you who she thinks you are?

Anger swells in my throat. What is that?

Authorized personnel only!

Fear pinches my nerves. What's going on here? Maybe I'm not such a unique situation. Maybe I'm not so special after all. Maybe there is something wrong with—

"The Toughest Kid in the World"

You are the toughest kid in the world. No one can outdo you in exercise, self-discipline, sheer will power, and losing weight. You are a Special Forces kid, the Green Beret and Navy SEAL of your time. Take pride in how special you are.

I stare blankly at the wall over Greta's shoulder. My mind is empty.

You are the best, aren't you?

Well, I . . . I . . . guess so. My mouth lets out another lion's roar yawn. Wow, I'm tired. I want a bed.

"Gary? Gary?" says Greta. "Are you okay? You look a little dazed all of a sudden."

"Huh? Oh—uh, I'm okay. I'm just a little tired, that's all."

Just Keep Smiling

I smile, smile, and smile some more, then yawn again. I wonder what meals are like up here. I won't be doing much walking this morning.

Lunch will be two bites.

I usually only have just an apple on Mondays. I wonder if I can get something like that for lunch. Come to think of it, I won't be doing the same exercise routine for the rest of the day.

Skip supper.

I suddenly become aware of a silence in the room. Greta and Mom look intently at me. Greta is grinning. Mom is scowling behind her smile.

"*Gaa*-ry!" says Mom, looking furious that I'm not paying attention. "Are you even hearing a word we're saying?"

Just nod and smile, Gary, just nod and smile.

I nod, feeling incredibly guilty.

Organizations to Contact

The editors have compiled the following list of organizations concerned with the issues debated in this book. The descriptions are derived from materials provided by the organizations. All have publications or information available for interested readers. The list was compiled on the date of publication of the present volume; the information provided here may change. Be aware that many organizations take several weeks or longer to respond to inquiries, so allow as much time as possible.

About-Face
P.O. Box 77665, San Francisco, CA   94107
(415) 436-0212
e-mail: info@about-face.org
Web site: www.about-face.org

About-Face's mission is "to equip women and girls with tools to understand and resist harmful media messages that affect self-esteem and body image." Based in San Francisco, the organization sponsors educational workshops for students as well as boycotts and other protests of companies that perpetuate unhealthy images of women. About-Face's online store offers humorous but provocative bumper stickers, postcards, and t-shirts that advance the organization's messages. The Web site also offers galleries of advertising "offenders" and "winners."

Academy for Eating Disorders
111 Deer Lake Road, Suite 100, Deerfield, IL   60015
(847) 498-4274 • fax: (847) 480-9282
e-mail: info@aedweb.org
Web site: www.aedweb.org

The Academy for Eating Disorders (AED) is a professional organization dedicated to promoting excellence in preventing, researching, and treating eating disorders. AED provides networking and collaboration opportunities for its members through its annual conference, publication of the *International Journal of Eating Disorders*, and an annual report of new developments in treatment research. The organization also undertakes advocacy projects, publishing position papers on issues such as the fashion industry's impact on eating disorders. For the public, AED's Web site offers a directory of its member clinicians and information on openings in current research trials.

Anorexia and Related Eating Disorders, Inc.
e-mail: jarinor@rio.com
Web site: www.anred.com

Founded in 1979, Anorexia and Related Eating Disorders, Inc. (ANRED) is a nonprofit organization that aims to help laypeople learn more about eating disorders and how to recover from them. ANRED's comprehensive Web site guides users through a series of more than fifty articles and resources covering definitions, statistics, risk factors, and recovery methods. In addition, the materials outline less-well-known eating disorders and explore the disorders' effects on specific populations.

The Body Positive
P.O. Box 7801, Berkeley, CA   94707
(510) 528-0101 • fax: (510) 558-0979
e-mail: info@thebodypositive.org
Web site: www.thebodypositive.org

The Body Positive endorses a health model called Health at Every Size, which promotes physical activity, good nutrition, healthy attitudes toward food, and positive body image as the best way to combat a variety of eating disorders. Founded in 1996, the organization sponsors school programs, seminars, and individual coaching. The Body Positive also supports creative outlets for exploring and coping with issues surrounding body image, body hatred, and body acceptance. The organization's publications include the *BodyTalk* series of

DVDs and curriculum materials as well as a book, *BodyAloud!*, which guides leaders through the development of their own body image curricula.

Eating Disorders Coalition for Research, Policy, and Action
720 7th Street, NW, Suite 300, Washington, DC   20001
(202) 543-9570
e-mail: manager@eatingdisorderscoalition.org
Web site: www.eatingdisorderscoalition.org

The Eating Disorders Coalition brings together a large number of professional and advocacy groups working together to raise public knowledge about eating disorders and to influence federal policy affecting eating disorders research and treatment. For example, the coalition has sought to expand health insurance coverage for the treatment of eating disorders and has fought to keep eating disorders at the center of the country's public health policy. The Web site lists upcoming events, reports on current legislative issues, and offers information on how individuals and groups can get involved in advocacy work.

Eating Disorders Information Network
124 Church Street, Decatur, GA   30030
(404) 816-3346
e-mail: info@myedin.org
Web site: www.myedin.org

The three-part mission of the Eating Disorders Information Network (EDIN) centers on education, outreach, and action. EDIN's educational components include curriculum materials for elementary schools through high schools. The organization emphasizes peer education programs and support groups. EDIN's outreach and advocacy programs include the M.O.D. Squad, a program to get mothers involved in promoting healthy body image and serving as balanced role models. The Atlanta-area organization sponsors an annual awareness walk and its free monthly newsletter is available online.

Eating Disorders Resource Center

2105 South Bascom Avenue, Suite 220, Campbell, CA   95008
(408) 559-5593 • fax: (408) 559-9515
e-mail: janiceb@healthtrust.org
Web site: www.eatingdisordersresourcecenter.org

Founded by a woman who has dealt with eating disorders for thirty years, the Eating Disorders Resource Center is dedicated to providing information and advocacy for patients, families, and the general public. The center is also committed to developing the next generation of activists and volunteers dedicated to the battle against these disorders. The Center's Web site offers a local support group for California's Silicon Valley region as well as a comprehensive list of national resources.

International Association of Eating Disorder Professionals

P.O. Box 1295, Pekin, IL   61555
(800) 800-8126
e-mail: iaedpmembers@earthlink.net
Web site: www.iaedp.com

An organization primarily for health care professionals working in the field of eating disorder research and treatment, the International Association of Eating Disorder Professionals (IAEDP) provides its members with opportunities for education and professional development. IAEDP offers a highly regarded certification program for nutrition and mental health professionals. It also publishes a newsletter, *Connections*, which outlines the latest advances in clinical research and treatment, and sponsors an annual symposium for its members.

National Association of Anorexia Nervosa and Associated Disorders (ANAD)

P.O. Box 7, Highland Park, IL   60035
(847) 831-3438 • fax: (847) 433-3996
Web site: www.anad.org

ANAD, the oldest eating disorder support organization in the country, was founded in 1976 by Vivian Meehan, a nurse and mother who had grown frustrated with the lack of available information on anorexia and other eating disorders. ANAD sponsors more than 350 free support groups worldwide for those affected by eating disorders. Consumer advocacy and education are also priorities for ANAD, which has lobbied for health care coverage of eating disorder treatment, pressured advertisers to promote healthy body types in the media, and fought against pro-anorexia Web sites. The ANAD Web site is available in English and Spanish.

National Association for Males with Eating Disorders, Inc.
e-mail: chris@namedinc.org
Web site: www.namedinc.org

Established in 2006 by Christopher Clark, who has himself experienced eating disorders, the National Association for Males with Eating Disorders, Inc. (NAMED) is the only nonprofit organization "exclusively dedicated to offering support to and education about males with eating disorders." Via its Web site, the association offers males and their families information about eating disorders, lists of relevant books and articles, and links to other resources.

National Eating Disorders Association
603 Stewart Street, Suite 803, Seattle, WA   98101
(800) 931-2237
e-mail: info@nationaleatingdisorders.org
Web site: www.nationaleatingdisorders.org

"Promoting public understanding of eating disorders and access to treatment" is the mission of the National Eating Disorders Association (NEDA). The organization sponsors a toll-free hotline and clinician referral service for those coping with eating disorders as well as a separate service for families and friends. Annual events include a national conference that brings together family members, health care providers, and activists for resource and information sharing, as well as National Eating Disorders Awareness Week, a public awareness event held each February. Publications include eating disorder and healthy body image curricula for schools and educational brochures.

Overeaters Anonymous
World Service Office, P.O. Box 44020
Rio Rancho, NM 87174-4020
(505) 891-2664 • fax: (505) 891-4320
e-mail: info@overeatersanonymous.org
Web site: www.oa.org

Like other twelve-step programs, Overeaters Anonymous (OA) focuses on regular meetings, sponsorship, and a recovery approach that addresses physical, emotional, and spiritual needs. OA sponsors about 6,500 weekly meetings around the world. It offers many publications, including its support magazine, *Lifeline*, which shares members' true stories of struggling with and overcoming compulsive eating. Other publications include twelve-step cards and brochures, inspirational pamphlets, resources for group leaders and sponsors, and support materials for family members. OA's Web site offers a directory of its meeting locations worldwide.

For Further Research

Books

Carrie Arnold, *Next to Nothing: A Firsthand Account of One Teenager's Experience with an Eating Disorder*. New York: Oxford University Press, 2007.

Lori Antosz Benson and Tara Leigh Benson, *Distorted: How a Mother and Daughter Unraveled the Truth, the Lies, and the Realities of an Eating Disorder*. Deerfield Beach, FL: Health Communications, 2008.

Carolyn Costin, *The Eating Disorder Sourcebook: A Comprehensive Guide to the Causes, Treatment, and Prevention of Eating Disorders*. New York: McGraw-Hill, 2007.

Julia K. De Pree, *Body Story*. Athens, Ohio: Swallow Press/ Ohio University Press, 2004.

Lauren Greenfield, *Thin*. San Francisco: Chronicle Books, 2006.

Trisha Gura, *Lying in Weight: The Hidden Epidemic of Eating Disorders in Adult Women*. New York: HarperCollins, 2007.

Betsy Lerner, *Food and Loathing: A Lament*. New York: Simon & Schuster, 2003.

Aimee Liu, *Gaining: The Truth About Life After Eating Disorders*. New York: Warner Books, 2007.

Courtney E. Martin, *Perfect Girls, Starving Daughters: How the Quest for Perfection Is Harming Young Women*. New York: Penguin Berkley, 2008.

John Morgan, *The Invisible Man: A Self-Help Guide for Men with Eating Disorders, Compulsive Exercise, and Bigarexia*. New York: Routledge, 2008.

Dianne Neumark-Sztainer, *I'm, Like, SO Fat!: Helping Your Teen Make Healthy Choices About Eating and Exercise in a Weight-Obsessed World*. New York: Guilford Press, 2005.

Nadia Shivack, *Inside Out: Portrait of an Eating Disorder*. New York: Atheneum, 2007.

Michael Strober and Meg Schneider, *Just a Little Too Thin: How to Pull Your Child Back from the Brink of an Eating Disorder*. Cambridge, MA: Da Capo Lifelong, 2005.

Gary Stromberg and Jane Merrill, *Feeding the Fame: Celebrities Tell Their Real-Life Stories of Eating Disorders and Recovery*. Center City, MN: Hazelden, 2006.

Kate Taylor, *Going Hungry: Writers on Desire, Self-Denial, and Overcoming Anorexia*. New York: Anchor, 2008.

Periodicals

Greg Archer, "Learning to Love Food Again," *O: The Oprah Magazine*, March 2008.

Fiona Bawdon, "No Model for Girls," *New Statesman*, October 1, 2007.

Cheryl Embrett, "Body Check," *Canadian Living*, November 2006.

Hannah Frankel, "A Dangerous Obsession," *Times Educational Supplement*, February 22, 2008.

Leslie Goldman, "Our Dirty Little Secret? We Can't Stop Bingeing," *Health*, June 2007.

Jessica Herndon and Michelle Tan, "'I Feel Grateful for Where I Am Now,'" *People*, April 21, 2008.

Hara Estroff Marano, "The Skinny Sweepstakes," *Psychology Today*, February 2008.

Anastasia Masurat, "Emaciated Online: Should Pro-Eating Disorder Groups Be Banned?" *Bitch: Feminist Response to Pop Culture*, Winter 2008.

Amelia McDonell-Parry, "Wanna Rexia," *Teen Vogue*, February 2008.

Jenni Schaefer, "The Lost Boys," *CosmoGirl!*, May 2007.

Hallie Levine Sklar, "Stay Away from the Fridge," *Good Housekeeping*, July 2007.

Lisa Turner, "What's Eating You?" *Better Nutrition*, June 2007.

Sally Wadyka, "Weighing In," *Vogue*, December 2006.

Index